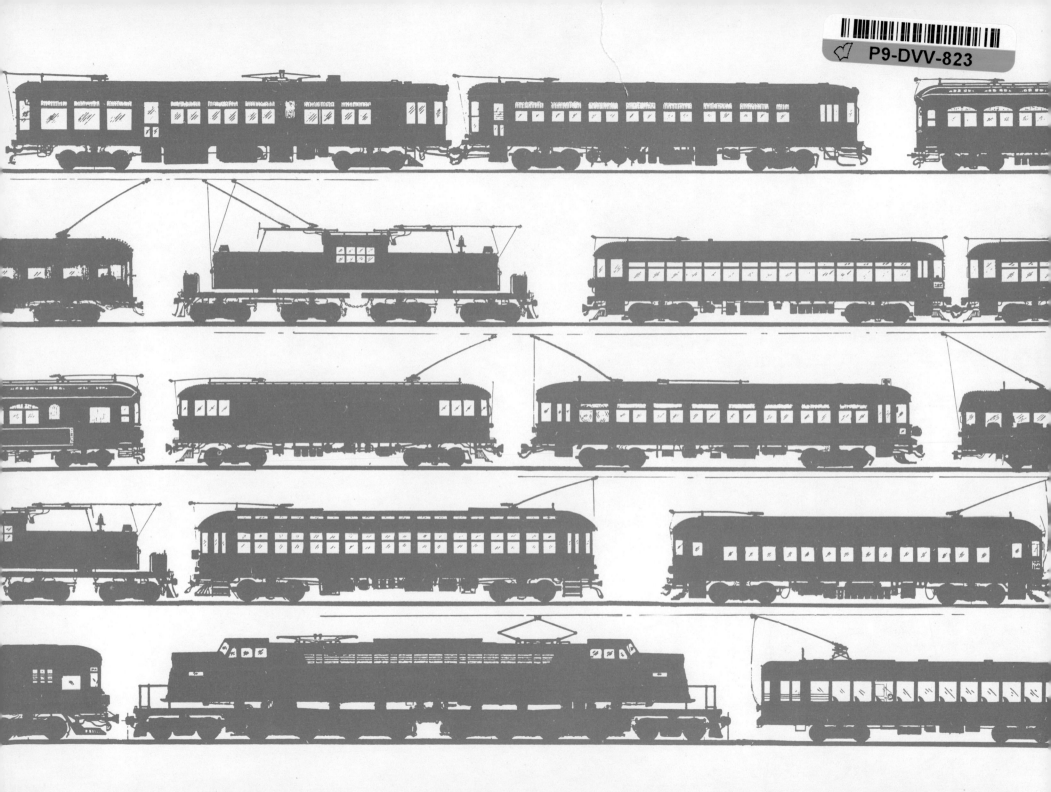

RED ARROW LINES

# A RAINBOW of TRACTION

Central Electric Railfans' Association

Bulletin 126

**TABLE OF CONTENTS**

# A RAINBOW of TRACTION

## Central Electric Railfans' Association

## Bulletin 126

# A RAINBOW OF TRACTION

Bulletin 126 of the Central Electric Railfans' Association

Copyright 1988 by the Central Electric Railfans' Association
All rights reserved
An Illinois Not-for-Profit Corporation
Post Office Box 503, Chicago, Illinois 60690, U.S.A.

Library of Congress Catalog Card Number 88-070492
International Standard Book Number 0-915348-26-8

CERA Bulletins are technical, educational references prepared as historical projects by members of the Central Electric Railfans' Association, working without salary due to their interest in the subject. This Bulletin is consistent with this stated purpose of the corporation: To foster the study of the history, equipment and operation of electric railways. If you can provide additional information, or are of the opinion that any statement herein is inaccurate or incomplete, please send documentation supporting such amendment or correction, citing sources, to the Central Electric Railfans' Association, P.O. Box 503, Chicago, Illinois 60690, U.S.A.

*A RAINBOW OF TRACTION* (B-126) was designed by George Krambles. Color separations and assembly are by Jim Walter Graphics Arts of Beloit, Wisconsin with typesetting by Guetschow Typesetting of South Beloit, Illinois. This book was printed by Sorg Printing Company of Illinois and bound by Zonne Bookbinders of Chicago, Illinois.

# ACKNOWLEDGMENTS

Among the publications CERA has issued during its half-century, the color albums present maximum opportunity for participation of individual members. As the list of contributors below and the dates on each photograph reveal, no other CERA books represent so many years of advance preparation by so many CERA members! Not so evident is the vast extent of reference material accumulated among the research team that was used to compile the texts of this book.

CERA founder George Krambles served as project foreman on this book. While CERA has long benefitted from his talents as a transit professional, editor, and pen-and-ink artist, it is the composite effort of the entire team which is responsible for the degree to which *A RAINBOW OF TRACTION* fulfills its objective of being accurate, usable and satisfying from historical, technical and photographic points of view.

Once again, this book contains a few short articles by our world observer, Jury Leonid Koffman, whose biography appeared in Bulletin 125. This time, Jury challenges us with some bits of theory with which engineers approach the solution of problems of performance and maintenance of electric trains. Jury's analyses demonstrate the value of including thorough review of past research and development work as input in working out new solutions to recurring issues, for example, those of ride quality, the effect of flange/tread contour, wheel steering, springing, etc. And he has equally penetrating insights into electric traction design ideas.

The editorial staff listed on the page opposite met at intervals, beginning even before CERA's previous book was off the presses, to begin the selection of photographs, starting with the overflow already on hand in reaction to the color albums *REMEMBER WHEN* and *The COLORFUL STREETCARS We Rode*. Color separations were ordered, reviewed and optimized. Caption research, a very much longer process than originally anticipated, followed. The sidebar technical articles and their diagrammatic illustrations were undertaken overseas. Assembly into a concept dummy was next. A combined team assignment was the extraction and compilation of the indices, which our readers recognize as a significant enhancement that began with CERA's previous book. Proofreading of conceptual draft text by each member of the editorial staff yielded dozens of refinements, corrections and additions. This step was new in this publication, separate from the more conventional proofreading of galley and signature flats. Lots of detail work, you'll agree, but essential ingredients of the quality control process for *A RAINBOW OF TRACTION*.

Contributors, in addition to the official CERA publications team, are listed below. Included are the photographers and individuals who provided answers to specific questions relating to the texts. The photographers are further identified, and (where known) the date and location, along the edge of each photo. Where two names are shown, the first is that of the original photographer, followed (in parentheses) by that person who supplied the photo for CERA use.

| | | | |
|---|---|---|---|
| R. R. Andrews | Bill Billings | C. A. Brown | F. E. Butts |
| N. D. Clark | R. L. Day | R. DeGroote | R. C. Gerstley |
| S. A. Goodrick | D. W. Harold | J. W. Higgins | L. K. Hill |
| G. H. Landau | T. A. Lesh | R. N. Lukin | G. G. McKinley |
| R. V. Mehlenbeck | W. D. Middleton | A. J. Schill | W. E. Schriber |
| J. P. Shuman | R. M. Stacy | H. Stange, Jr. | E. Van Dusen |

and posthumously:

| | | | |
|---|---|---|---|
| A. R. Alter | W. B. Cox | T. H. Desnoyers | S. D. Maguire |

*Norman Carlson*
for the CERA publications team

Chicago, October 1988

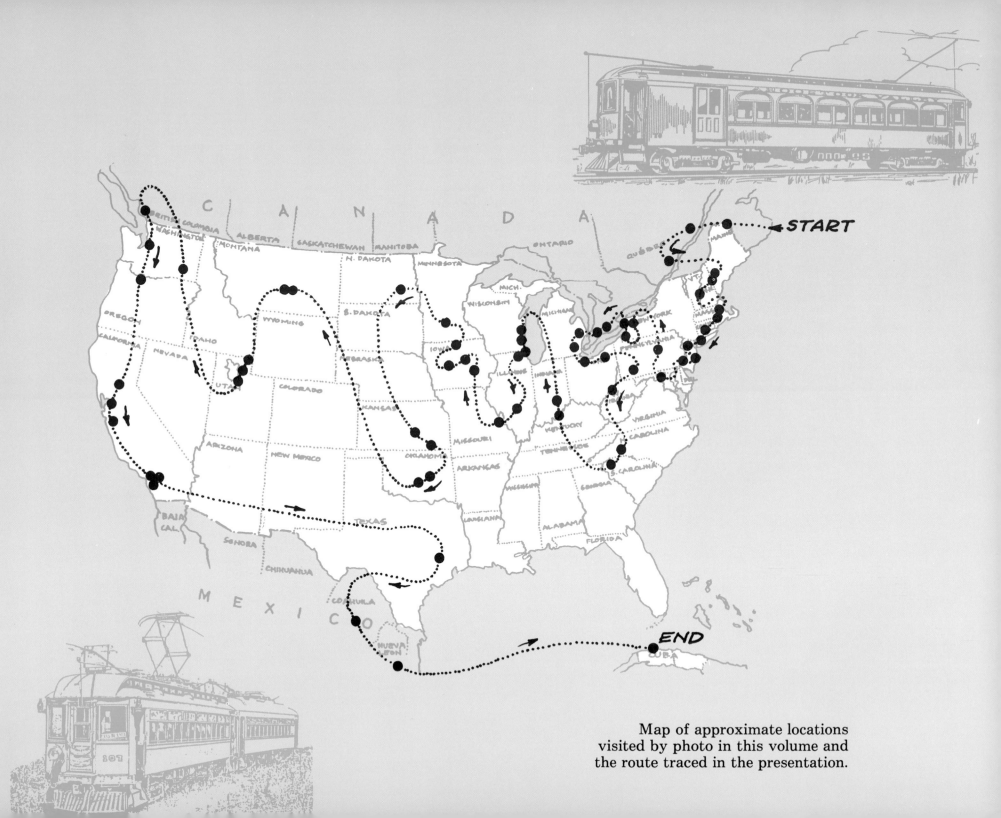

START

END

Map of approximate locations
visited by photo in this volume and
the route traced in the presentation.

# A RAINBOW OF TRACTION

With this book, CERA commemorates its golden anniversary. In May of 1938 a modest four-page publication was issued as a hand-out on a farewell trip over the Gary Railways line to Valparaiso, Indiana, a trip which sparked the creation of the Central Electric Railfans' Association and one of its major activities, the publication of technical, educational, historical reference material about electric rail transportation.

*RAINBOW* completes a trilogy of full-color volumes that illustrate the development of electric railways. It covers the interurban railways, rapid transit lines, switching and main line railroad electrifications in North America based on available color photographs taken between 1939 and 1964.

The presentation follows a meandering path illustrated by the map on the facing page, starting in the northeast corner of Maine, criss-crossing the United States and Canada to the far southwest and then returning through Mexico to end in Cuba. To help you, there is provided a very concise summary of the history and a few technical features of each property illustrated, along with some key specifications of the vehicles shown.

Since color photography was costly and undependable in the middle 1930s, and really only became practical and widely available for the amateur after World War II, the rarity and quality of much of the work shown here is truly remarkable. The reader will note particularly the names of those railfan color photography pioneers memorialized by this book.

CERA was an early experimenter in the color reproduction, going back nearly thirty years, but the possibilities in this field have only become within the reach of amateur publications such as ours with modern developments in color separation and offset printing technology. As an example of the kind of equipment needed to produce this work, there is the $200,000 laser scanner which was available for Bulletin 126 for the first time.

As has been the case with CERA's previous color albums, we hope and expect that this one will trigger readers to check their collections for unusual and historical material for future publication. And of course there will be more use of color to illustrate the quarter century since as well as the future developments marking a renaissance in electric rail transportation.

R. L. DAY / July 14, 1945 / Washburn, ME

## AROOSTOOK VALLEY RAILROAD 71

Presque Isle-Washburn, ME ................... (+) July 1, 1910
Washburn-Sweden-Caribou, ME ............ (+) 1911-1912-1913 in steps
Sweden branch ............................ (−) late 1930s
Freight service dieselized ................. (−) July 12, 1945
Caribou-Presque Isle ..................... (−) August 7, 1946
(Only switching track at Presque Isle retained thereafter)

Miles of line ................................ 34
Power system .............................. 1200 v DC trolley
Passenger motor cars, all time ............... 4
Vehicle series shown ........................ 70 - 71
Length over all ............................. 53 ft.

Weight in tons .............................. 32
Motors, quantity / builder / rating ........... 4 / GE-217A / 50 hp
Control, single or double end / type ......... DE / GE-K42A
Approximate free speed ..................... 35 mph
Builder / year delivered .................... Wason / 1912

Having much of the appearance of a midwestern interurban, Aroostook Valley was a railroad treasure in the extreme northeast corner of the United States, serving the Maine countryside. One trainman, Granville "Granny" Allen, made the three daily-except-Sunday round trips, collecting fares, handling pouch mail and throwing switches, as well as driving. Running time one way was a leisurely sixty minutes.

Cars 52, 70 and 71 are preserved at the Seashore Trolley Museum.

## AROOSTOOK VALLEY RAILROAD 53

Vehicle series shown . . . . . . . . . . . . . . . . . . . . . . . . . . . . . 53
Length over all . . . . . . . . . . . . . . . . . . . . . . . . . . . . . . . . . 32 ft.
Weight in tons . . . . . . . . . . . . . . . . . . . . . . . . . . . . . . . . . . 40
Motors, quantity / builder / rating . . . . . . . . . . . . . . . . . 4 / GE 205B / 100 hp
Control, single or double end / builder / type . . . . . . . . DE / GE / M
Approximate free speed . . . . . . . . . . . . . . . . . . . . . . . . . 25 mph
Builder / year delivered . . . . . . . . . . . . . . . . . . . . . . . . . General Electric / 1911

This railroad's meager passenger potential was supplemented early on by serving freight traffic, including the region's famed potato crop. This steeple cab motor was later superseded for basic freight duty by #54, a Baldwin-Westinghouse 60-ton engine, and #53 became a snow fighter and relief locomotive.

G. KRAMBLES / August 6, 1957 / Limoilou, Quebec, Canada

## CANADIAN NATIONAL RAILWAYS 226

Formerly Quebec Railway Light & Power

| | |
|---|---|
| Quebec - St. Joachim electrified in stages | (+) 1900 |
| Sold to Canadian National Railways | (+) 1950 |
| Discontinued passenger service | (−) March 15, 1959 |
| Freight dieselized | (−) April 1959 |

| | |
|---|---|
| Miles of line | 25 |
| Power system | 600 v DC trolley |
| Locomotives owned | 6 |
| Vehicle series shown | 226 - 227 |
| Length over all | 41 ft. |
| Weight in tons | 67½ |

| | |
|---|---|
| Motors, quantity / builder / rating | 4 / |
| Control, single or double end / type | DE / |
| Approximate free speed | 30 mph |
| Builder / year built | National Steel / 1918 |
| Acquired from / year | Hydro Elec Pwr Comm. / 1924 |

This short line served as a suburban feeder to the Quebec city system, but also as an access route for a Canadian National Railways weekday through train between Quebec and Murray Bay (La Malbaie), an 88-mile trip, with a QRL&P locomotive handling the movement west of St. Joachim.

An interesting peculiarity of QRL&P was the continued use of stub switches into the 1950s.

A. J. SCHILL / May 29, 1967 / Montreal, Quebec, Canada

## CANADIAN NATIONAL RAILWAYS 186
Montreal terminal and suburban services

| | |
|---|---|
| Montreal - St. Eustache and branches | (+) 1914, as Canadian Northern Railway |
| Miles of line | 27 |
| Power system | 2400 v DC catenary |
| Motor passenger cars / locomotives, 1967 | 6 / 18 |
| Vehicle series shown | 180 - 188 |
| Length over all | 40 ft. |
| Weight in tons | 101 |

| | |
|---|---|
| Motors, quantity / type / rating | 4 / Dick Kerr 96 / 430 hp |
| Control, single or double end / type | DE / English Elec camshaft |
| Approximate free speed | 35 mph |
| Builder / year delivered | Engl. El.-Beyer Peacock / 1924-26 |

An early instance of British rolling stock in North America was provided for the waterfront electrification of Montreal's harbor. Phased out in 1940, these engines were obtained for suburban service over the old Canadian Northern through Mount Royal tunnel where, along with similar GE American-built motors, they have set longevity records.

11

N. D. CLARK / May 21, 1955 / Montreal, Quebec, Canada

Montreal-St. Lambert-Longueuil, St. Lambert-
Marieville, in steps ........................ (+) Oct. 1909 - Sept. 1913
Marieville-St. Cesaire-Granby, in steps .......... (+) May 1914 - Apr. 1916
Granby, rerouted from street to CNR .......... (±) Jan. 2, 1925
Marieville-Ste. Angele ...................... (+) Jan. 6, 1926
Montreal South-Longueuil .................... (−) 1932
Marieville-Granby de-electrified .............. (−) Nov. 24, 1951
(Diesel service continued by CNR)
Montreal South-Montreal .................. (−) June 19, 1955
(Electric service continued St. Lambert-Marieville, with connecting
service Montreal-St. Lambert given by Canadian National Railway
diesel train)
All remaining electrified track ................. (−) October 14, 1956

| | |
|---|---|
| Miles of line (1951) .................... | 51 |
| Power system ........................... | 600 v DC catenary |
| Passenger motor cars owned, 1951 ................ | 43 |
| Vehicle series shown .................... | 102 - 105 |
| Length over all ......................... | 49 ft. 4 in. |
| Weight in tons .......................... | 28.5 |
| Motors, quantity / builder / rating .............. | 4 / Wh 306 / 60 hp |
| Control, single or double end / type............. | DE / Wh HL 189D |
| Approximate free speed ................. | 40 mph |
| Builder / year delivered ................. | Ottawa / 1912 |

The Montreal entrance of this suburban/interurban railway was a tortuous single track with railroad grade crossings and street running in mixed traffic. Most critical was the drawbridge crossing the Lachine Canal, known as Black's Bridge, which when opened to allow a ship to pass would invariably cause monumental delay.

The three miles of single track between Montreal terminal and East End in St. Lambert included only one passing siding, West End, at its midpoint, with a capacity of 15 cars. To get the passenger traffic over this section of line in rush periods, it was *de rigueur* to operate trains in platoons, with extra sections of some of them, all on the same schedule. For example in timetable 70 of August 1951, at 4:27 PM, seven eastbound trains met three westbounds here. With extra sections in some of both the eastbounds and westbounds, there was a mighty exchange of whistle signals!

*(margin, rotated) PAUL B. CARS*

## INTERURBAN CAR SUSPENSIONS

Experience has shown that static deflection of an interurban truck suspension should be about ⅝" for every 10 mph. Of this, some 20%-30% should be allocated to the axlebox and the rest to the bolster assembly. The overall damping factor of hydraulic dampers should be $D = 0.4$ of the critical aperiodic value between truck frame and axle boxes. The effective length of swing link (or equivalent suspension devices) should be at least 12" while the damping of the truck to body suspension should be about $D = 0.25$ of the critical for tare conditions. The springs and damping mechanisms should yield a natural frequency of body bounce of about 1.45 Hz not persisting longer than 2.5-3.0 cycles.

Similarly 12" links not affected by friction or with their effective length reduced by differences of the radii at the points of support, should have a natural frequency of about 1 Hz and should come to rest after about 1¾ cycles due to the damping in the horizontal plane.

Frequency and damping properties can be readily determined in both planes. In the vertical plane, the car is placed on 1"-1½" wedges so that all wheels drop simultaneously onto the rails, thus exciting the natural frequency of body bouncing oscillations. Mechanical or electrical recordings indicate the natural frequencies as well as the damping values. In the lateral plane, the car body is pulled sideways on the truck from attachment points as near as possible to the height of the body center of gravity.

Simultaneous release, effectively achieved by the use of electric bomb-release locks borrowed from the nearest military airfield, provides the records of the frequency and decay of the lateral oscillations and thus confirms the effective link length and damping properties of the bolster assembly.

J. L. K.

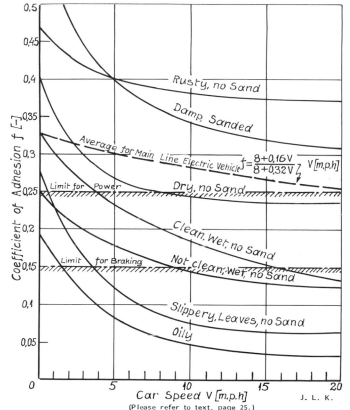

(Please refer to text, page 25.)

An adhesion value of 0.25 has been experimentally proven appropriate for street and interurban railway operation up to 25 mph. Above that, main line adhesion values are applicable in motoring mode. In braking, 0.15 adhesion should be used at all speeds. Adhesion values for street and interurban cars should be considered at up to 25 mph with main line values applicable at higher speeds. For braking $f = 0.15$ should be considered as the limit at all speeds.

R. L. DAY / September 17, 1949 / Sanford, ME

▲ YORK UTILITIES COMPANY 108-100-102

| | | | |
|---|---|---|---|
| Sanford-Springvale, ME via Main St. | (+) Feb.-May 1893 | | |
| | (−) Apr. 2, 1935 | | |
| Sanford-Springvale, ME via River St. | (+) December 7, 1923 | | |
| Passenger service discontinued | (−) April 1, 1947 | | |
| To Sanford & Eastern & dieselized | (−) June 1949 | | |
| Totally abandoned | (−) 1961 | | |

| | | | |
|---|---|---|---|
| Miles of line (1940s) | 2.4 | | |
| Power system | 600 v DC trolley | | |
| Vehicle series shown | 108 | 100 | 102 |
| Length over all | 36'-8" | 34'-0" | |
| Weight in tons | 22½ | 23 | 23 |
| Motors | 4-GE70 | 4-GE80 | 4-GE80 |
| Control | K28d | K35G2 | K28f |
| Builder | Laconia | Laconia | Laconia |
| Year delivered | 1905 | 1906 | 1906 |

(108 originally Portsmouth Dover & York, acquired 1923)

At one time Atlantic Shore Line Railway, predecessor of York Utilities, operated a 52-mile system linking Springvale to several towns along the Atlantic coast. It served nearly five million riders in 1915.

The short Sanford-Springvale segment outlasted all other electric railways in Maine, except for that of the Seashore Trolley Museum in Kennebunkport, where YU cars 100 and 108 are preserved today.

CLAREMONT RAILWAY 18 ►

| | |
|---|---|
| W. Claremont-Claremont-Claremont Jct., NH | (+) Aug. 16, 1903 |
| Claremont-Claremont Jct., and passenger service | (−) May 7, 1930 |
| Dieselized and sold to Claremont & Concord Ry., | (−) 1955 |

| | |
|---|---|
| Miles of line | 5 |
| Power system | 650 v DC trolley |
| Locomotives owned at time of photo | 2 |
| Vehicle series shown | 18 |
| Length over all | 26 ft. |
| Weight in tons | 32 |
| Motors, quantity / builder / rating | 4 / GE-57 / 50 hp |
| Control, single or double end / builder | DE / General Electric |
| Approximate free speed | 20 mph |
| Builder / year delivered | GE / 1907 |

A rarity among the electric railways in New England, this one was able to interchange freight cars with connecting main line railroads and, as a result, survived long after most of its contemporaries. It served mills, machinery and shoe factories, most of which have since relocated in southern states or abroad. As a result total abandonment is now a possibility.

R. L. DAY / January 23, 1946 / Springfield, VT

## SPRINGFIELD TERMINAL RAILWAY 16

| | |
|---|---|
| Springfield, VT-Charleston, NH | (+) August 1, 1897 |
| Passenger service discontinued | (−) January 11, 1947 |
| Freight service changed to diesel | (−) October 31, 1956 |

| | |
|---|---|
| Miles of line | 8 |
| Power system | 550 v DC trolley |
| Passenger cars | 2 |
| Vehicle series shown | 16 - 17 |
| Length over all | 42 ft. |
| Weight in tons | 22 |
| Motors, quantity / builder / rating | 4 / GE-265 / 35 hp |
| Control, single or double end / type | DE / GE-K35 |
| Approximate free speed | 37 mph |
| Builder / year delivered | Wason / 1925 |

This little railway remained important as the link to the American rail network via the Boston & Maine Railroad, even though it had a difficult alignment, with 4% grades and 125 ft. radius curves, winding continuously to follow the Black River. More recently it has gained fame by lending its name to the entire system acquired by the Guilford interests, who made its less restrictive work rules applicable to an otherwise dying system of branch line railways.

After passenger service ended, but while electric operation remained, car 16 was retained by STR for utility purposes. Along with STR8, 10 & 12, it was acquired in 1956 by the trolley museum at Warehouse Point, CT.

S. A. GOODRICK / 1954 / Springfield, VT

## SPRINGFIELD TERMINAL RAILWAY 06 ▲

| | |
|---|---|
| Vehicle series shown | 06 |
| Length over all | 40 ft. |
| Motors, quantity / builder / rating | 4 / GE-80 / 40 hp |
| Control, single or double end / type | DE / GE-K28 |
| Builder / year delivered | Wason / 1913 |
| Acquired from / year | Bangor Ry & El No. 106 / 1942 |

This car was used as a maintenance of way unit for the remaining life of STR's electric operation. It was scrapped in 1957.

## BOSTON REVERE BEACH & LYNN R.R. 6-100 class ► ▲

| | |
|---|---|
| East Boston-Lynn, MA | (+) July 29, 1875 (steam) |
| Winthrop loop | (+) 1884 - 1888 (steam) |
| East Boston-Lynn electrified | (+) October 19, 1928 |
| Winthrop loop electrified | (+) November 15, 1928 |
| Entire system closed | (−) January 27, 1940 |

| | |
|---|---|
| Miles of line | 13 |
| Power system | 600 v DC catenary or trolley |
| Motor cars owned | 64 |
| Vehicle series shown | 6-100 |
| Length over all | 58 ft. 0 in. |
| Weight in tons | 26 |
| Motors, quantity / builder / rating | 2 / GE-295A / 60 hp |
| Control, single or double end / type | DE / GE M C-305 |
| Approximate free speed | 35 mph |
| Builder / year delivered | Laconia / 1905 |

In the gathering clouds of the Great Depression when this 36-inch gage suburban line decided to electrify, instead of buying state-of-the-art cars, it retrofitted some of its open-platform wooden coaches which were actually behind the times when built back in 1905. But they are said to have been great fun as an amusement ride. The early abandonment was hastened by the phasing out of Boston El's Atlantic Avenue line and the interconnecting ferry service. Ten years later, rapid transit was extended from Maverick station north into the same territory using some BRB&L right-of-way.

17

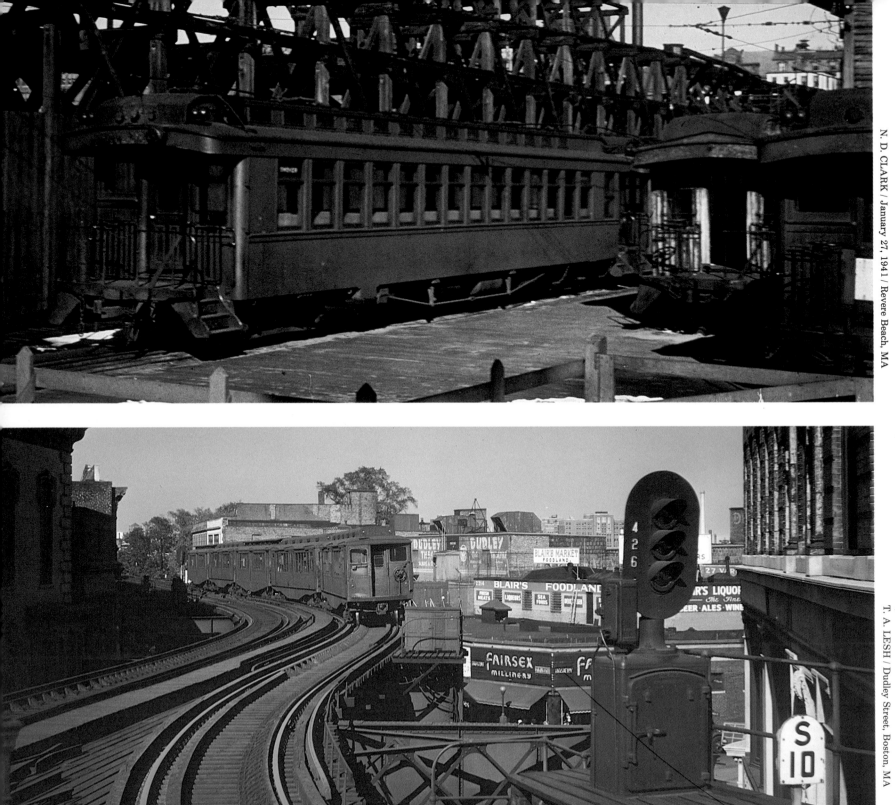

N. D. CLARK / 1956 / Taftville, CT

◄ BOSTON ELEVATED RAILWAY 0901 class
Main Line Elevated (MBTA's Orange Line)

| | |
|---|---|
| Sullivan Square-Forest Hills | (+) 1901-1909 in steps |
| Sullivan Square-Everett | (+) 1919 |
| Replaced/extended Oak Grove-Forest Hills | (+) 1975-1987 in steps |
| Miles of line | 12 |
| Power system | 600 v DC 3rd rail |
| Motor cars at time of photo | 218 |
| Vehicle series shown | 0901-0967 |
| Length over all | 46 ft. 11 in. |
| Weight in tons | 47 |
| Motors, quantity / builder / rating | 2 / Wh-301 / 175 hp |
| Control, single or double end / type | DE / Wh-ALM - C26 |
| Approximate free speed | 40 mph |
| Builder / year delivered | Laconia / 1907 |

The south terminal of Boston's first rapid transit line was originally here at Dudley Street in Roxbury. A fascinating complex of various levels of street car and elevated railway tracks, it had very short radius loops for turning trains as well as ramps and loops for the street cars, and later, buses.

Today, operation through the Roxbury community is along the former New Haven Railroad via Back Bay instead of on elevated structure above the streets.

PONEMAH MILLS COMPANY 1 ▲

| | |
|---|---|
| Electrified switching of mill trackage | (+) 1894   (−) 1964 |
| Miles of line | Approx. 1 |
| Power system | 500 v DC trolley |
| Vehicle series shown | 1 |
| Length over all | 24 ft. |
| Weight in tons | 35 |
| Motors, quantity / builder / rating | 4 / LWP20 / 125 hp |
| Approximate free speed | 20 mph |
| Builder / year delivered | Thomson-Houston (GE Lynn Works) / 1894 |
| Acquired from / year | Cayadutta Elec. R.R. / 1895 |

This was a pioneer electric locomotive, attracting much attention at the time it was built, by incorporating features such as an enclosed cab and the basic concept of the center steeple cab, giving the motorman a commanding view in either direction.

The engine was preserved and after an uncertain period was acquired by the Connecticut Electric Railway Trolley Museum at Warehouse Point, CT.

G. H. LANDAU / March 1964 / Rye, NY

## NEW YORK NEW HAVEN & HARTFORD R.R. 304 (Class EF4)

| | |
|---|---|
| New York (Woodlawn) NY-Stamford, CT electrified | (+) 1907 |
| Stamford-New Canaan, CT electrified | (+) 1908 |
| Bronx-New Rochelle, NY electrified | (+) 1912 |
| Stamford-New Haven, CT electrified | (+) 1914 |
| South Norwalk-Danbury, CT electrified | (+) 1925 (−) 1945 |

| | |
|---|---|
| Miles of line | ± 104 |
| Power system | 11 kv 25 hz catenary, except 600 v DC third rail while on New York Central below Woodlawn |
| Multiple unit cars / locomotives, 1962 | 362 / 22 (estimated) |
| Vehicle series shown | 300 - 311 |
| Length over all | 69 ft. 6 in. |
| Weight in tons | 174 |
| Motors, quantity / builder / rating | 6 / GE-752 / 750 hp |
| Control, single or double end / type | DE / GE Ignitron rectifier |
| Approximate free speed | 65 mph |
| Builder / year delivered | General Electric / 1956 |
| Acquired from / year received | Norfolk & Western 230-class / 1963 ex Virginian Ry. 230-class |

After N&W took over, and then shut down, the Virginian electrification, New Haven is said to have bought these "hi-tech" engines for a distressed price of only $25,000 each! Later, as New Haven switched to diesel power for freight, the same engines served both Penn Central and Conrail as 4600-4610.

They were retired in 1981. CR 4604 was donated to the Roanoke Museum of Transportation, to be restored as VGN 135. CR 4600 (renumbered 4601-II) is also saved, at Connecticut Valley Railroad Museum.

## NEW YORK NEW HAVEN & HARTFORD R.R. 377 ►

| | |
|---|---|
| Vehicle series shown | 370 - 379   Class EP-5 |
| Length over all | 68 ft. |
| Weight in tons | 174 |
| Motors, quantity / builder / rating | 6 / GE-752F / 660 hp |
| Control, single or double end / type | DE / GE PCL |
| Approximate free speed | 90 mph |
| Builder / year delivered | Alco-GE / 1955 |

Ordered for high-speed passenger service to operate between New Haven and either Grand Central or Pennsylvania stations in Manhattan, the EP-5s could take power from either the 11 kv 25 hz New Haven overhead or New York Central's 650 v DC on underrunning or overhead 3rd rail. It was planned that they continue in service under Penn Central management as 4970-4979, but only 371, 373-377 did so, becoming PC 4971, 4973-4977. These have now been supplanted under Amtrak on runs through Pennsylvania station by AEM-7 locomotives.

## NEW YORK NEW HAVEN & HARTFORD R.R. 4021 ►

| | |
|---|---|
| Vehicle series shown | 4020 - 4023 |
| Length over end sills | 69 ft. 6 in. |
| Weight in tons | 87 |
| Motors, quantity / type / rating | 4 / Wh 156 / 170 hp |
| Control, single or double end / type | DE / Wh AB-26A |
| Approximate free speed | 50 mph |
| Builder / year delivered | Standard Steel / 1909 |

Few American suburban railroads adopted the open platform coach body like this early New Haven commuter car. Extreme in their weight due to having to carry control gear for both the New Haven 11 kv AC and New York Central 650 v DC systems, these 4000s could nevertheless lumber along with two or three similar trailers.

They are, of course, long supplanted by vestibule equipment, and those in turn, have been superseded by modern high-performance M2 and M4 types.

J. P. SHUMAN / September 3, 1967 / West of New Haven, CT

R. C. GERSTLEY / Ca 1947 / New Haven, CT

21

▲   LONG ISLAND RAIL ROAD 1317 (Class MP70)

Began operation as a steam railroad, 1835
Electrified suburban New York portions in stages, mostly 1905-1926.
  Although some branches have been abandoned, further extension of
  electrification continues, most recently Hicksville-Ronkonkoma on
  January 18, 1988.
Diesel powered push-pull trains are used on non-electrified lines.

| | |
|---|---|
| Miles of line electrified | ± 150 |
| Power system | 650 v DC overrunning 3rd rail |
| Motor cars owned (1986) | 935 |
| Vehicle series shown | 1301 - 1350 |
| Length over all | 80 ft. 8½ in. |
| Weight in tons | 79 |
| Motors, quantity / rating | 2 / Wh-559 / 225 hp |
| Control, single or double end / type | DE / Wh ABF XMA63 |
| Approximate free speed | 62 mph |
| Builder / year delivered | Pennsylvania R.R. Altoona / 1948 |

   The double-deck car was developed in the effort to increase passenger capacity per foot of train. This version had a full length corridor from which one stepped down to the lower seats or stepped up to the upper seats. Complaints of dirt and immodesty made them unpopular and led to the adoption of the 85 ft. car with 3-2 transverse seating in today's 100% modern high performance fleet.

NEW YORK CENTRAL SYSTEM 114   ► ▲

Electrification for access to Grand Central Terminal, Manhattan
New York City to Croton and Mott Haven to

| | |
|---|---|
| White Plains, in steps | (+) 1906-1913 |
| Sedgwick Av-Getty Square | (+) 1926 (−) 1943 |
| Melrose-Port Morris (freight only) | (+) 1926 (−) Ca 1955 |
| Spuyten Duyvil-30th St. | (+) 1931 (−) Ca 1955 |
| Operation taken over by Metro North (MTA) | (±) January 1, 1983 |
| N. White Plains-Brewster | (+) April 30, 1984 |
| Miles of line at the peak | 75 |
| Power system | 650 v DC underrunning and overhead 3rd rail |
| Locomotives at peak ownership | 166 |
| Vehicle series shown | 101 - 134 ex 1101 - 1134 ex 3201 - 3234 ex 3401 - 3434 |
| Length over all | 38 ft. 9 in. |
| Weight in tons | 114 |
| Motors, quantity / builder / rating | 4 / GE-84A / 550 hp |
| Control, single or double end / builder / type | DE / GE / M |
| Approximate free speed | 70 mph |
| Builder / year delivered | Alco-GE / 1906 |

   The landmark electrification and Grand Central Terminal project of the New York Central & Hudson River Railroad inaugurated an era, with innovations such as underrunning third rail and gearless motor drive. The distinctive styling of these class S motors was adopted to ease retraining steam locomotive enginemen, used to driving from behind the boiler.
   Only three straight electric locomotives remain today on this electrification, their place having been taken over by dual-power diesel/electrics and by Metro North's imposing fleet of modern high-performance MY cars whose design was overseen by late MCERA Arthur Raabe.

# THE SNAKEPATH OF THE INTERURBAN

Rough riding of some interurban cars was often attributed to poorly laid or inadequately maintained track. This liveliness, mainly related to the horizontal plane, is usually referred to as hunting, snaking or nosing.

Reasons for this oscillating motion, often considered unavoidable though capable of constraint, have been known for a long time. In 1883 a senior official of the Wurttenburg State Railways, Oberbaurat Klingel, provided a detailed analysis of what happened when a single wheelset with conical tire treads proceeded on a straight track path. Admittedly a single wheelset is not of much use under service conditions but the axlebox-to-axleguard clearances usually present in conventional trucks are perfectly adequate to permit free wheelset movement within the confines of the total flange-to-rail clearance.

Because of tread conicity the two wheels of a set scarcely ever roll on identical diameters and since both are rigidly coupled by the axle, the wheel rolling on the greater diameter will cover a greater distance causing the set to turn by a small angle about its vertical axis, steering it towards the rail at the opposite wheel. This forces the opposite wheel to proceed on a greater radius steering the set back towards the opposite rail and forcing the wheelset to pursue a wavelike motion down the track. This is the path dealt with by Klingel, referred to as the sinusoidal or wavelike motion.

Klingel calculated the "Length of the complete Snakeline" as determined by the wheel radius, the tire conicity and the distance between the rolling circles of the two wheels. From this, the frequency of the motion exciting the lateral oscillations could be determined and the buildup of unpleasantly intense body oscillations was avoided by appropriate modifications to the suspensions provided between the car body and the trucks. Over a century ago Klingel stressed that "Cylindrical tires have been used on a number of occasions but these were discarded time and again because it was found that their use resulted in a decisive running of the flanges up against the rails causing a substantial increase of the wear of both". Furthermore, "The outlook for the success of the application of cylindrical tires is therefore very small."

"Slightly conical treads appear to be of considerable advantage at least on lines with numerous straight sections which can be negotiated at high speeds. . . . The elongation of the snakeline will be of considerable benefit as far as smooth running is concerned by extending the impulses of lateral displacement over greater time intervals. This will

slow down the motion which will in turn check its intensity". However in spite of Klingel's arguments, quite a few railroads including the Chicago North Shore and Milwaukee would not give up hope, the latter causing quite a stir with the use of cylindrical treads some 40 years after Klingel's warnings, while others tried their luck with loose wheels only to drop these as soon and as quietly as possible.

The next step in the search for better riding qualities was along the lines indicated by Klingel, i.e., "elongating the snakepath". The challenge was taken up in 1887 by the grand old man of railway engineering Royal Railway Construction and Operations Inspector Boedecker at Hannover, followed in 1896 by Marie in France, 1916 by Carter in England and Ruegger in Switzerland, 1933 by Mauzin in France and in 1934 by Kreissig in Germany. In 1935 Rocard in France and in 1937-1940 Heumann in Germany showed that the wavelength of the wheel motion can be substantially extended by guiding the wheelsets in the horizontal plane in a rigidly framed truck.

The resultant elongation is determined by the truck wheelbase and the distance $2s$ between the rolling circles of the wheels. For standard gauge with $2s$ — 4'11" and a 6' wheelbase truck, the elongation factor $E$ will be 1.49.

According to Klingel the wavelength of the snakepath due to standard gauge 26" wheels with 1:10 treads amounts to 32.45' which at 50 mph will provide a lateral excitation frequency of 2.26 Hz. Positively located wheelsets would reduce this to about 1.5 cycles per sec.

On the other hand, tests carried out by Professor Krettek on articulated car #405 of the Siegburg-Siebengbirgs Interurban showed that with chevron rubber axlebox spring units as widely used with European street interurban and rapid transit stock, the forces emanating from the wheelsets were able to overcome the spring resistance at speeds in excess of about 25 mph. This enabled the excitation frequencies due to the trucks to jump from elongated to free wheel values. However, at speeds above about 50 mph more complex interaction between wheels and rails intervenes to slow down the rise of excitation frequencies to the benefit of riding qualities.

As far as vehicle design is concerned, the art is to avoid resonance conditions between the excitation frequency originating at the trucks and that of the car body carried by the swing links, flexicoil springs or equivalent arrangements. The swing link frequency is

$$f = 3.14 \sqrt{1/\text{L Hz}},$$

where $L$ is the effective link length in inches. Here it would be advisable to choose a link length with resonance at relatively low vehicle speeds rarely used for any length of time, or one at which resonance would be attained at speeds well above the highest envisaged limits. Generally it would be desirable to uncouple the body from the trucks so that truck hunting motion can't readily be transmitted to the body and to have long swing links or equivalent devices. Thus the effectively same 12" long swing links of some Brill trucks would insure a natural frequency of 0.9 Hz which with standard gauge 6' wheelbase trucks and tread slope at 1:10 would result in resonance at about 20 mph with free (and at about 30 mph with positively located) wheelsets, a desirable arrangement with vehicles required to operate at higher speeds. However, vehicles for lower speeds would benefit from the use of 1:20 treads which would reduce the nosing frequency to 0.7 of the above value so that resonance conditions would be encountered acceptably at about 14 or 21 mph respectively.

It should be mentioned, however, that original tread conicity alters with wear and this affects the excitation frequency. One remedy a tread profile similar to the worn shape so that the excitation pattern will not be altered by wear. This also increases the intervals between wheel turning and preserved the cold rolled tread and flange surfaces.

Such considerations were mainly responsible for the development and rapid spread of a variety of truck designs incorporating positively located wheelsets. An early form of this design is represented by the equalizer truck referred to as the swan-neck, MCB or Pennsylvania design with which the wheelsets are coupled by the swan-necked equalizer beams.

J. L. K.

◄ ◄ NEW YORK CENTRAL SYSTEM 4523

| | |
|---|---|
| Motor cars, 1950 | 234 |
| Vehicle series shown | 4500 - 4599 |
| Length over all | 85 ft. 0 in. |
| Weight in tons | 75½ |
| Motors, quantity / builder / rating | 4 / GE-1240 / 100 hp |
| Control, single or double end / type | DE / GE-KG113A3 |
| Approximate free speed | 50 mph |
| Builder / year delivered | St. Louis / 1950 |

This design of suburban MU car adapted the typical main line railroad streamlined coach body and styling to the special requirements of dense commuter service. Incongruous appearing rattan-covered 3-2 seating served 130 passengers per car. These cars, which were renumbered 1000-class by Penn Central, are now replaced by high performance M-1 stainless steel cars brought on line by MTA's Metro North division. A few of the 1000s have gone on to Cuba for use as diesel-hauled coaches.

## ADHESION

Although the performance of an interurban train depends on adhesion between wheel and rail, the mostly singly operated cars were rarely required to accelerate rapidly, pull heavy loads or negotiate steep inclines, so the actual adhesion values did not matter all that much. When it came to braking what there was seemed to suffice and as speeds increased braking could be enhanced by the use of magnetic track brakes.

Main line railroads were more concerned with braking, particularly when, as speeds increased, signal spacings could not be altered correspondingly. Here extensive road tests established that, to avoid slip or slide, the coefficient of adhesion (the ratio of the force $f$ between wheel and rail in the direction of motion to the static wheel load) should not exceed

$$f = 0.15.[1]$$

This corresponds to a retardation of 4.8 ft/sec² (3.3 mph/sec). This rate is accepted by the transit industry as adequate for service conditions and acceptably comfortable for standing passengers.

Similar values are seldom exceeded when it comes to acceleration either, but an adhesion $f = 0.15$ is not sufficient to deal with trailing loads. The added static wheel load of trailers sharply reduces the overall coefficient of adhesion. In starting, this adverse effect is worsened by the power car rearing about the coupler and the trucks transferring some axle load from the front to the rear wheels. Usable tractive effort is thus limited by what the front wheels of the leading truck can do without spinning. It is here that adhesion values become decisive, especially where electric locomotives with up to 1500 hp per axle are concerned. Numerous adhesion tests over the years have resulted in development of multinotch control, softer suspensions (ensuring steadier riding with less pronounced pitching, bouncing, and swaying) and checking weight transfer from front to rear by suitable truck-to-body attachment designs.

Recent progress to stepless chopper or variable-frequency-variable-voltage (VVVF) microprocessor-controlled propulsion is a further contribution to increased adhesion as indicated in this table:

Adhesion (% of weight on drivers) at 25-50 mph speeds

| Rail condition | Conventional resistor control | Chopper or VVVF control |
| --- | --- | --- |
| Dry | 0.25 | 0.40 |
| Wet | 0.22 | 0.30 |

Street and interurban railways remained more modest both as far as testing and achievement were concerned. Here adhesion values of up to 0.25 are appropriate for tangent track up to 25 mph, paying attention to the trailing loads, nowadays often shared between the end power trucks of articulated cars. At higher speeds main line adhesion values are applicable. The fact that as speeds increase adhesion values drop due to wheel slip, spin or creep triggered by vehicle oscillations excited by the track must be taken into account in the relevant aspects of track and car design.

As an example, standard gauge 26″-36″ diameter wheelsets with treads having 1:20 taper and a total flange-to-rail clearance of ½″, passing through a 100 ft radius curve will have the outer wheel traveling the equivalent of 5.2% farther than the inner one. The outer flange running up against the rail will increase the friction at the point of contact but on the other hand the tendency to lift the tread off the rail reduces adhesion. All of this too deserves consideration in the design of vehicle and track.

As far as braking is concerned an adhesion value of 0.15 should not be exceeded. To combat wheel spinning when starting or running up grades sand is commonly used, especially for emergency braking, even though as a side effect it adds wear and tear on axle guides, bearings, and electrical equipment, and may interfere with good shunting of signal circuits.

Drivers early discovered another useful technique to control slipping: when accelerating on slippery rails and faced with wheel spinning, instead of sanding or switching off and notching up once more, they would quickly but gently apply the hand brake to check the spinning and enable the wheels to restore the required adhesion.

This simple but effective remedy was also used during the early days of electric traction on the Gotthard main line in Switzerland. At first, this practice had been prohibited, as it seemed irrational to apply the brakes at the very instant when high tractive effort was needed! Later, after it was appreciated that the use of sand brought maintenance problems, locomotives were fitted with "spinning wheel brakes" (Schleuderbremse). With these wheel spinning indicated by the motor ammeters or by a warning light was checked by the driver pressing a button to actuate a quick-acting valve which charged or discharged the brake cylinders (within a second or less) to a brake shoe pressure corresponding to 15 to 20% of the axleload. Ideally, it would be desirable to accord this treatment only to the wheelsets involved, but the demand for simplicity led to a common application to all wheels. This also cleaned and dried all treads. An alternative approach developed in France rapidly reduced and then restored power to traction motors to get a similar effect. Nowadays a solid state version of this latter concept is commonly used for modern slip-slide mitigation.

J. L. K.

1 The actual coefficient of *rolling friction* for steel wheel on steel rail is commonly accepted to be about 25% dependably, but the coefficient of *sliding friction* is less. Therefore, the shortest stopping distance (and the best accelerating) is achieved when working at the rolling adhesion limit and avoiding slip or slide.

NEW YORK CITY TRANSIT AUTHORITY — MUDC TRAIN   ► ▲
Third Avenue L line, Chatham Sq. — Gun Hill Rd.,
Service discontinued May 12, 1955

| | |
| --- | --- |
| Miles of line, 1954 | Approx. 13 |
| Power system | 600 v DC overrunning third rail |
| Vehicle series shown | 1613 - 1652 |
| Length over all | 48 ft. |
| Weight in tons | 36 |
| Motors, quantity / builder / rating | 2 / GE 66 / 125 hp |
| Control, single or double end / type | DE / GE-M |
| Approximate free speed | 37 mph |
| Builder / year delivered | Barney & Smith / 1910 |

The last L line in Manhattan is seen in its final days when its riders had been presumably weaned away to the newer IND subways paralleling, but several long blocks to the west. Service in peak hours was still a hefty 17 local and 28 express trains with about 250 cars in peak hours, but there was no night or weekend service.

Wooden cars like these, used in local service, were originally open platform "gate" cars that had been rebuilt about 1924 with Multiple Unit Door Control, hence the group classification, MUDC.

S. D. MAGUIRE / 1954 / 34th St. on Third Ave. L, New York City

N. D. CLARK / April 3, 1959 / Brooklyn, NY

### NEW YORK CITY TRANSIT AUTHORITY Corona Yard ▲
Route 7 Flushing service

| | | |
|---|---|---|
| Miles of line | 10 | |
| Power system | 600 v DC overrunning 3rd rail | |
| Vehicle series shown | 8570-9306 | 9307-9769 |
| Exterior color 1964 | red | blue |
| NYCTA type (contract) designation | R29, R33 | R33, R36 |
| Length over all | 51 ft. 4 in. | 51 ft. 4 in. |
| Weight in tons | 37 | 37 |
| Motors, quantity / builder / rating | 4 / GE-1240 / 100 | 4 / Wh1447 / 100 hp |
| Control | GE-17KC76 | Wh-XM 379 |
| All are single end cars in married pairs, except 9306-9345 are double end single cars | | |
| Approximate free speed | 50 mph | 50 mph |
| Builder | St. Louis | St. Louis |
| Year delivered | 1963 | 1964 |

The 7 Flushing line of the New York subway system is one of its most important and productive routes. Eleven-car trains are operated in the peak. Much of the elevated portion of the line through Queens is triple-tracked so that express service can be provided in the rush direction.

The Flushing and Astoria routes of today's NYCTA were built to the Interborough (IRT) narrow profile loading gage by the city for joint use of the IRT and BRT (later BMT, Brooklyn-Manhattan) rapid transit companies, each of which had three services from Manhattan using them at one time. The Astoria line was modified about 1947 to accommodate the standard wide BMT equipment. The Flushing line, by then extended from Corona to Flushing, was rerouted from Queensboro Plaza via the so-called Steinway tunnel and subway to a terminal at Times Square.

### ◄◄ SOUTH BROOKLYN RAILWAY 4

| | | |
|---|---|---|
| Brooklyn waterfront-Coney Island | (+) 1904 | |
| De-electrified | (−) 1962 | |
| Miles of line | 9 | |
| Power system | 600 v DC trolley | |
| Locomotives operated at time of photo | 4 | |
| Vehicle series shown | 4 | |
| Length over all | 31 ft. | |
| Weight in tons | 57 | |
| Motors, quantity / builder / rating | 4 / Wh-508 / 25 hp | |
| Approximate free speed | 20 mph | |
| Builder / year delivered | Brooklyn R.T.Co. / 1907 | |

The South Brooklyn Railway is a surface railroad partly under the Culver elevated rapid transit line, connecting docks along New York Bay with Coney Island main shops of today's NYCTA, its owner. As a common carrier, at one time it served a number of industries along the route.

The home-built motor was renumbered by NYCTA to 20001, but was taken out of service when an air reservoir exploded and blew a hole through the roof. It was renumbered 4 and now is preserved in the trolley museum at Branford, CT.

S. D. MAGUIRE (G. KRAMBLES) / May 20, 1956 / Morristown, NJ

▲ ◄ PENNSYLVANIA R.R. 1213-1212, class MP52
Hudson & Manhattan sevice, "K"-class

33rd St. (NYC) - Hoboken, NJ
Hudson Terminal (NYC) - Newark, NJ
Hoboken-Grove St.-Exchange Pl., NJ
Grove Street-Newark, NJ . . . . . . . . . . . . . . . . . . . . . . (+) In steps 1908-1912
The portion between Journal Square and Newark was Pennsylvania R.R.;
    the remainder was built by Hudson & Manhattan R.R., which operated
    the rapid transit service over the whole.
Line relocations were made by Pennsylvania R.R. to shift Newark
    terminal from Park Place to Penn Station and in Manhattan by PATH
    to accommodate the change from former Hudson Terminal to today's
    World Trade Center.

| | |
|---|---|
| Miles of line | 14 |
| Power system | 650 v DC overrunning third rail |
| Motor cars owned at time of photo | 447 |
| Vehicle series shown | 1206 - 1229 |
| Length over all | 51 ft. 3 in. |
| Weight in tons | 34½ |
| Motors, quantity / builder / rating | 4 / GE-1250A / 100 hp |
| Control, single or double end / type | SE / GE MCM |
| Approximate free speed | 70 mph (short field) |
| Builder / year delivered | St. Louis / 1958 |

The Hudson & Manhattan, including its Newark extension, was taken over by Port Authority Trans Hudson, a public agency, on September 1, 1962. In 1963, three of the "K" cars, including the 1213, were scrapped. In 1967 the remaining "K" cars were leased and given PATH markings. Conrail became their owner.

◄ ◄ STATEN ISLAND RAPID TRANSIT RY. CO. 326

| | |
|---|---|
| Steam railroad | |
| St. George Ferry-Tottenville, NY | (+) April 13, 1860 |
| Portions Electrified | |
| St. George-Clifton-S. Beach | (+) June 25, 1925 |
| Clifton-Tottenville | (+) July 1, 1925 |
| St. George-Port Ivory | (+) December 25, 1925 |
| Passenger services abandoned | |
| Clifton-South Beach | (−) 1953 line torn up |
| St. George-Port Ivory | (−) 1953 de-electrified |
| Miles of line | 23 |
| Power system | 650 v DC overrunning 3rd rail |
| Motor cars owned at time of photo | 90 |
| Vehicle series shown | 300 - 389 |
| Length over all | 67 ft. |
| Weight in tons | 48 |
| Motors, quantity / builder / rating | 2 / GE-282A / 200 hp |
| Control, single or double end / type | DE / GE PC-10 |
| Approximate free speed | 50 mph |
| Builder / year delivered | Standard Steel / 1925 |

Since 1971 the Tottenville line has been a unit of the Metropolitan Transit Authority (MTA). It is an isolated line, a surface railway using subway technology. It was built as an independent steam railroad and had been acquired by the Baltimore & Ohio Railroad as a means of reaching piers in the Clifton-Stapleton area.

Suburban passenger traffic developed. With the possibility of linking it to the Brooklyn subway system via a proposed tunnel below the Narrows, B&O selected car and infra-structure standards fully compatible with BMT.

◄ ◄ DELAWARE LACKAWANNA & WESTERN R.R. 2359 - 2614
Electrified suburban lines

| Began electrified service: | Miles | | |
|---|---|---|---|
| Hoboken-Newark-Summit-Gladstone, NJ ....... | 42 | (+) | September 3, 1930 |
| Summit-Dover................................ | 20 | (+) | September 3, 1930 |
| Newark-Montclair............................ | 4 | (+) | September 3, 1930 |
| Combined to form Erie-Lackawanna, then acquired by Conrail. | | | |
| Acquired by New Jersey Transit Rail Operation .. | | (+) | April 1982 |
| Electrification converted to 25 kv 60 hz ......... | | (+) | Sept. 16, 1984 |
| Dover-Netcong ............................. | 8 | (+) | |

| | |
|---|---|
| Miles of line, 1956 ......................... | 67 |
| Power system, 1956 ......................... | 3000 v DC catenary |
| Motor cars, 1956 ........................... | 141 |
| Vehicle series shown (motor car).................. | 2500 - 2641 |
| Length over all.............................. | 70 ft. 3½ in. |
| Weight in tons .............................. | 73½ |
| Motors, quantity / builder / rating ............... | 4 / GE-750A / 235 hp |
| Control, single or double end / type............... | SE / GE-PC |
| Approximate free speed ....................... | 67 mph |
| Builder / year delivered ....................... | Pullman / 1930 |

The 1930 electrification of Lackawanna's suburban service was another precedent setting occasion, with the adoption, after a long series of developmental tests at the GE East Erie plant, of the 3000 v DC system. Trains were made up of two-car semi-permanently coupled motor-trailer sets, using all new motor cars and a mix of rebuilt and new trailer coaches. The details above are given for the motor cars.

Although it certainly paid for itself over a half-century life, it was not adaptable to integration into the long range objectives of New Jersey Tansit. A number of the old green cars have been preserved in rail museums across the country.

## THE AC (ALTERNATING CURRENT) INTERURBANS

The majority of the world's main line railways have utilized alternating currents, originally 16-2/3 or 25 Hertz (Hz) frequency. Why did not the otherwise modern, technically thrusting though financially sparing, interurbans make wider use of the advantages claimed for alternating current electrification?

Proponents of AC electrification could claim a power distribution system using simple "static" substations. With high trolley voltage easy to obtain, an AC system, with light trolley overhead, could feed vehicles over greater distances. In this respect AC was simpler and markedly less expensive than the then predominating DC systems. With DC, trolley voltage, ordinarily in the 500-700 range, was limited to about 3000 by difficulties with motors and switchgear. On the other hand, early AC motors were heavy and performed poorly with arcing commutation. There was also a problem with adhesion, resulting from pulsating torque. Discounting both the sweeping claims for AC, advanced at the time by Westinghouse interests and no less vehement opposition by the DC-oriented Edison influenced group, by the turn of the century traction motors of adequate power suitable for operation on low frequency AC were evolved.

The development of AC traction commutator motors was of fundamental importance to the evolution of railway electrification. The basic principle of the single-phase traction motor is the same as that of the direct current series motor. With AC power, as the direction of the current is reversed the direction of rotation and torque is not altered, since the polarity of armature and field magnets is reversed simultaneously during successive half-cycles. A direct current series motor could operate on alternating current if it were not for excessive heating produced by eddy currents and

hysteresis losses in the poles, yoke and armature. To reduce these the entire magnetic circuit of the alternating current series motor is laminated and the iron used is of a type having low hysteresis losses.

However, such a motor exhibits a number of additional drawbacks: it runs slower, it sparks, and it vibrates intensely, particularly when starting. Both the sometimes rather vicious sparking at the brushes and the overheating of certain armature coils are due to the relatively large circulating currents induced by the alternating main flux in the coils short circuited by the brushes. These coils and the main field coils act as the secondary and primary windings of a transformer. Thus the magnetic field flux affects not only the field coils, but also the armature coils. These are short circuited by the brushes covering two or more commutator bars at the very instant of commutation, which results in generating a "transformer sparking tension" which is at its highest at the brushes, the current flow closing via the brushes by entering from one commutator segment at one brush edge and leaving via the other.

The current intensity depends mainly on the resistance at the contact area between the brush and the commutator segments, since compared with this the resistance of the armature coils is of secondary importance. This contact resistance depends on the current density and it falls with the increase of the latter so that at about 100 Amp/sq cm the transition voltage approaches a terminal value of about 2.5V. At higher values, contact becomes intermittent and a further rise leads to the glowing of the brushes. As the current transfer flow heats the brushes the resistance drops and current rises, heating the brushes still further. Because of this it is advisable to limit the short circuit voltage to about 3.5 to 4 when starting and to 2.5 to 3V at the one-hour load.

The consequences of heavy short circuit current cause torque to become periodically negative, and the gear loses contact only to gain it again in a somewhat jerky manner.

Such rotor vibrations adversely affect brush action. Brushes have a small clearance in their holders to permit expansion and to prevent seizure due to dust deposits, thus permitting a certain degree of fore-and-aft motion due to armature oscillations. The resultant brush tilting causes these to contact the commutator with one or the other edge only which reduces the number of short circuit armature coils. The oscillating armature motion scrapes carbon dust off the brushes and this heated up by the passing current, glows, producing a rather intense stream of sparks.

Due to the drive of George Westinghouse (1846-1914) whose face for many years adorned the cases of a well-known German cigar, "Der Hanseate", (the Hanseatic businessman) the AC motor problem was solved by Benjamin Garver Lamme, Westinghouse's chief engineer. The solution was effective and in its overwhelming simplicity at a par with Sprague's trolley wheel and axle-hung motor.

In a paper presented in New York to the American Institute of Electrical Engineers on September 26, 1902, Lamme reported the creation of the first reliable single-phase traction motor. His solution was to introduce a resistance in the path of the circulating current between armature coils and the commutator segments and to reduce the number of the coils short circuited then by the use of narrow, high resistance brushes covering two segments only. The novel resistances were inserted between the junctions of the armature coils and the commutator segments. They were located either at the bottom of the slots with the armature windings or between the front of the armature connections and the commutator segments. The short circuit current was forced to flow from one armature coil through the resistance and brush on through the other resistance bar to the adjacent coil. The current kept as low as required by suitable choice of resistance values. Since the current flowed through these resistances only during the short circuit interval of the armature coils concerned, the resultant losses became much smaller. The Lamme solution was of great interest, particularly since at that time the prospects of ever developing a suitable AC commutator traction motor appeared to be rather bleak.

Since the short circuit current generated in the armature coils is directly proportional to the power frequency, this had to be kept low. In Europe, a frequency of 15 Hz was considered as desirable, since, compared with one of 25 Hz, this would reduce losses in the overhead trolley and the rail return. This in turn permitted wider substation spacing. Furthermore, the inductive voltage drop in the motors could be reduced by some 50% and the power factor improved by 5%, so that the motor costs could be reduced by up to 30%. The low frequency would be inaudible should any of it be induced in the telephone network. On the basis of these considerations, a number of European railways decided in favor of 15 Hz, later standardizing on 16-2/3 Hz as one-third of the general commercial power frequency of 50 Hz.

In the U.S.A., 60 Hz became the generally adopted commercial power frequency, although in the early days there was also much power generated at the industrial frequency of 25 Hz. The latter was nearly universally used for AC interurban overhead. Visalia Electric opted for 15 Hz at the time and consideration was being given to large scale AC electrification of the Southern Pacific Railroad throughout the west coast region. Westinghouse lost no time in advocating wider application to the rapidly growing interurban networks. The main advantages stressed at the time related to the reduced number of substations which, in addition to being some 40% less costly than the DC equivalent, did not require attendants. The lighter overhead distribution would permit an increased distance between line poles. Furthermore, the Lamme motor permitted running over DC streetcar lines.

In summary, the advantages claimed in favor of AC equipment were: less costly power stations and distribution lines, fewer and unattended substations, reduced maintenance requirements, reduced energy losses, better power plant utilization due to commercial demands of adjoining communities, lower motor voltage, and loss-free multistep speed control. On the other hand, the use of AC motors, transformers and switchgear, as well as the main grid resistors required to permit running under DC as well as AC overhead resulted in markedly increased car weights, increased first costs, maintenance expenses of rolling stock, track and adjoining pavement in city streets.

First to avail himself of AC electrification for interurban operation was Charles L. Henry (1849-1927) who, educated as a lawyer, served for four years in the Indiana State Senate. He was to be subsequently elected for two terms as a Representative in Congress. In 1891 he acquired and electrified a street car line in Anderson, Indiana, which he extended 11 miles to Alexandria.

Henry is credited with coining the word "interurban" to describe the rural electric railway. Further extensions and amalgamations of his starter line led to the creation of the Union Traction Company of Indiana, which in 1902 was absorbed by the Schoepf-McGowan interests, leaving Henry free to concentrate on the construction of the Indianapolis & Cincinnati Traction Company. This connected Indianapolis with Greensburg (49 miles) and Connersville (58 miles) and was to be extended to Cincinnati. Between 1904 and 1907 the lines were equipped by Westinghouse with a 2 x 500 kw 25 Hz power station and 33000 V feeder lines, substations and the 3300 V AC overhead, as well as the equipment for twenty 4 x 75 hp, 44.5 t, 55 seat, WC and baggage compartment cars, originally limited to 45 but later remotored aiming at 60 mph. The cars were provided with bow current collectors for the AC lines while trolley poles were used over street car lines. The AC system was retained only until 1924 when it was replaced by a 600 V DC supply and new rolling stock.

Following this "first", both Westinghouse and General Electric supplied AC equipment to nineteen interurbans embracing over 1,000 miles, the length of the individual lines ranging from 15 to 140 miles. Most of these were equipped between 1904 and 1908 changing to the simpler and operationally less expensive 600 to 1200 V DC supply between 1910 and 1921. Only one, the San Francisco Napa and Calistoga Railway, remained AC-powered throughout its life from 1905 to 1937.

Whatever the shortcomings of the early AC interurbans, and there were many, these were in no small way caused by the need to run over street railway lines. The required additional equipment, as well as special operating procedure, could scarcely endear the new system to users rightly expecting utmost simplicity and reliability. Frequently quoted data relating to advantages secured by the Washington, Baltimore and Annapolis Railway by changing within two years from 6600 V AC to 1200 V DC are not entirely convincing, since long, heavy and complex cars were replaced by shorter and lighter ones permitting through-city running. Yet there is little doubt that the AC system, still in its infancy, could not compete with the fully developed DC equipment,

particularly when it came to the requirements of the city centers served lines. Even so, the optimism shown at the time ultimately resulted in important developments originating with modest interurbans which pointed the way to a pattern of main line electrification adopted by most of the world's railways. With development of solid state power-conditioning systems such as those using the gate-turn-off thyristor, AC distribution seems assured of growing popularity in the future.

J. L. K.

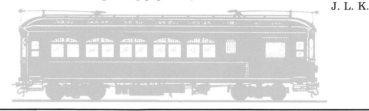

PENNSYLVANIA RAILROAD 1 ► ►
Electrified portions (per condensed summary below)

| Segment | AC | DC | (+) | (−) |
|---|---|---|---|---|
| Long Island RR NY, parts of | | *x | 1905 | |
| Dillsburg-Mechanicsburg, PA | | °x | 1906 | 1926 |
| Penn Station-Manhattan Tfr. NY-NJ | | *x | 1910 | 1935 |
| Philadelphia-Paoli, PA | x | | 1915 | |
| Philadelphia-Chestnut Hill, PA | x | | 1918 | |
| Philadelphia-White Marsh, PA | x | | 1924 | |
| Philadelphia-Westchester, PA-Wilmington, DE | x | | 1928 | |
| Philadelphia-Norristown, PA | x | | 1930 | 1960 |
| Philadelphia-Trenton, NJ | x | | 1930 | |
| Trenton-New York (Sunnyside) | x | | 1933 | |
| Wilmington, DE-Washington, DC-Potomac Yard, VA | x | | 1935 | |
| Paoli-Harrisburg, PA main line | x | | 1938 | |
| Harrisburg, PA-Perryville, MD | x | | 1938 | 1970s |
| Harrisburg-Lancaster-Parkesburg, PA | x | | 1938 | 1970s |

| | |
|---|---|
| Miles of electrified route (1958) | 675 |
| Power system | DC° = 600 v side trolley |
| | DC* = 600 v overrunning third rail |
| | AC = 11 kv 25 hz catenary |
| Vehicle series shown | 1 - 7 |
| Length over all | 73 ft. 9 in. |
| Weight in tons | 264 |
| Motors, quantity / builder / rating | 6 / GE-290A / 550 hp |
| Control, builder / type | Double end / GE - PCL |
| Approximate free speed | 20 mph, fully loaded 55 mph maximum |
| Builder / year delivered | Alco-GE / 1927 |
| Acquired from / year | Great Northern Ry / 1956 |

When the Great Northern's Cascade tunnel in Washington state was modified to permit diesel operation, PRR acquired this type of locomotive and assigned it as helpers for slow-moving freights working east out of Enola Yard, Harrisburg. The design was a break-through in technology, using motor-generators to convert 11 kv AC catenary input to 1500 v DC to feed the traction motors. In Pennsylvania service they were superseded by class E-44. Since Conrail takeover freight operation has been dieselized over what remains of this once-great electrification.

PENNSYLVANIA RAILROAD
Above:    Class MP54
Below:    Class MP85      Head car 153

| | ►▲ | ►► |
|---|---|---|
| Vehicle class | MP54 | MP85 |
| Vehicle series shown | 409 - 799 | 150 - 155 |
| Length | 64 ft. 5¾ in. | 85 ft. 0 in. |
| Weight in tons | 65 | 45 |
| Motors, quantity / type / rating | 2/Var/200 hp | 4/Wh1454A/100 hp |
| Control, single or double end / type | DE/WhAB | DE/WhAB |
| | | ignitron |
| Approximate free speed | 65 mph | 65 mph |
| Builder / year delivered | Var/1910-27 | Budd/1958 |

In the systematic, incremental way Pennsylvania Railroad had for developing its equipment designs, the mechanical and electrical features of the MP54 electric suburban car evolved over a forty year span without changing the basic body design.

Then came a breakthrough in the middle 1950s with the stainless steel MP85 "Pioneer III" cars. The original series shown served as production prototype for the higher performance Silverliner design which ultimately totally replaced the classic MP54s. The Pioneers were renumbered 294-299 in 1968, then 244-248 in 1974, 199 having been destroyed by fire in the meantime.

Gap and Gordonville are rural communities a few miles east of Lancaster, PA, outside the fast expanding Main Line suburban sprawl of greater Philadelphia.

32

J. P. SHUMAN / Ca 1954 / Gap, PA

J. P. SHUMAN / July 6, 1958 / Gordonville, PA

J. P. SHUMAN / 1965 / Safe Harbor, PA

### PENNSYLVANIA R. R. 4419 and 4450  ▲

| | | |
|---|---|---|
| Vehicle series shown | 4400-4465, exc. | 4438-4459 |
| | Class E44 | Class E44a |
| Length over all | 69 ft. 6 in. | 69 ft. 6 in |
| Weight in tons | 192 | 195 |
| Motors, quantity / builder / rating | 6/GE752/733 | 6/GE752/833 hp |
| Control, single or double end / type | DE/GE ignitron | DE/GE silicon |
| Approximate free speed | 70 mph | 70 mph |
| Builder / year delivered | General Electric / 1960-1963 | |

The class E44 was a sturdy workhorse for heavy freight service and advanced the use of rectifier technology on locomotives by the change to silicon rectifiers in the course of production of the 66-unit order. Its adoption made possible the elimination of helper locomotives on the heavy grades east of Harrisburg.

Nevertheless, Pennsylvania successor Conrail replaced all electric freight operation with diesel power by November 22, 1979. Engines 4458-4465 went to New Jersey Transit in 1983 but after sitting about unused until 1987, went on to Amtrak for use (as numbers 500-507) in work train service on the Northeast Corridor. The remainder were traded back to General Electric for diesel power.

### PENNSYLVANIA RAILROAD 4743  ► ▲

| | |
|---|---|
| Vehicle series shown | 4743-4754 |
| | Class P5A modified |
| Length over all | 62 ft. 8 in. |
| Weight in tons | 180 |
| Motors, quantity / builder / rating | 6 / Wh 425 or GE-A625 / 625 hp |
| Control | Double end |
| Approximate free speed | 70 mph |
| Builder / year delivered | Baldwin-Westinghouse / 1935 |

This railroad developed, in cooperation with General Electric and Westinghouse, distinct designs for its electrification, working its way through some developmental prototypes. The first extensive production model was the P5, of which some 92 were built. The first run had box cabs with end driving cabs, but the Loewy-designed stream-lined body with centrally located cab soon followed. This provided more protection for the engine crew and became the pattern adopted for 139 GG1s. As they came on line, the P5s were geared down and reassigned to freight service, as on this triple-headed coal drag.

### PENNSYLVANIA RAILROAD 4912  ► ►

| | |
|---|---|
| Vehicle series shown | 4800-4938 |
| | Class GG-1 |
| Length over all | 79 ft. 6 in. |
| Weight in tons | 238½ |
| Motors, quantity / builder / rating | 6 / GE-A621 or A622 twin / 385 hp per armature or 4620 hp total |
| Control, single or double end / type | DE / tap-changer + buck-boost |
| Approximate free speed | 100 mph |
| Builder / year delivered | PRR-BLH-GE-Wh / 1935-1941 |

For a half-century the Pennsylvania R.R. GG-1 ruled the Northeast Corridor. That it occupied the pinnacle of electric locomotive design world wide was without doubt due to the cooperative R & D program of PRR and its suppliers which preceded manufacture.

However, its record included a few experiences guaranteed to try anyone's soul, like the train brakes failing when 4876 arrived at Washington Union Terminal in January 1953. It charged through the bumping post into the concourse, crashing through the floor into the baggage room below. It could be removed only by dismantling into pieces less than six feet in any dimension. Nevertheless, Altoona shops reassembled it and returned it to service by November!

A wide variety of equipment from many owning and operating companies could always be seen in the busy yard at the west end of Pennsylvania Station, Manhattan, New York. This view looks northwest. The main lines to Philadelphia, Washington and Chicago via the Hudson River tunnel are in the center of the layout, with westbound GG1 and eastbound P54 consists.

(Photo: W. C. Janssen / October 4, 1957)

F. J. GOLDSMITH, Jr. / August 31, 1940 / Atlantic City, NJ

**ATLANTIC CITY & SHORE RAILROAD 106 ▲**
(Shore Fast Line division)

| | |
|---|---|
| Atlantic City-Somers Point, NJ ............... | (+) August 25, 1906 |
| Somers Point-Ocean City .................... | (+) 1907 |
| Atlantic City-Ocean City .................... | (−) January 18, 1949 |
| Miles of line ............................... | 16 |
| Power system............................... | 650 v DC trolley and overrunning third rail |
| Motor cars owned at time of photo ......... | 20 |
| Vehicle series shown ....................... | 101 - 117 |
| Length over all ............................ | 47 ft. 1 in. |
| Weight in tons ............................. | 35 |
| Motors, quantity / builder / rating ......... | 4 / GE-87 / 60 hp |
| Control, single or double end / type......... | DE / GE / M |
| Approximate free speed .................... | 40 mph |
| Builder / year delivered .................... | Stephenson / 1906 |

Shore Fast Line was an important feeder to owner West Jersey & Seashore Railroad, part of the Pennsylvania System.

The train is shown on Atlantic Avenue at Arkansas on its way to Ocean City from the terminal on Virginia Avenue at the famous boardwalk.

The portion of this line powered by third rail was West Jersey & Seashore trackage that had once carried MU electric trains through to Camden, NJ.

**READING COMPANY 301  ► ▲**
Philadelphia-Jenkintown-Doylestown-
Hatboro-Nottistown-Chestnut Hill-

| | |
|---|---|
| West Trenton, PA .......................... | (+) July 26, 1931 |
| Miles of line ............................... | 69 |
| Power system............................... | 11 kv 25 hz catenary |
| Motor cars owned at time of photo ......... | 130 |
| Vehicle series shown ....................... | 300 - 306 |
| Length over all ............................ | 72 ft. 11½ in. |
| Weight in tons ............................. | 63 |
| Motors, quantity / builder / rating ......... | 2 / GE-620 / 300 hp |
| Control, single or double end / type......... | DE / GE ABM |
| Approximate free speed .................... | 72 mph |
| Builder / year delivered .................... | Bethlehem Steel / 1931 |

The last major suburban railroad system to be electrified was that of the Reading Company in the Philadelphia region. This system is now integrated into the Southeastern Pennsylvania Transportation Authority, a multi-modal system.

A very few of these original heavy-weight MUs, rebuilt to straight coach configuration, currently remain in service.

W. C. JANSSEN / May 9, 1966 / Jenkintown, PA

PHILADELPHIA SUBURBAN TRANSPORTATION CO. 80 ► ▲

Suburban trolley lines, 62½ in. gage,
   radiating from 63rd Terminal, then
   the Philadelphia City Limits, to
   West Chester, Media, Ardmore and
   Sharon Hill . . . . . . . . . . . . . . . . . . . . . . . (+) 1899-1917 in stages
Terminal changed from 63rd to 69th . . . . . . . . . (−) April 30, 1907
West Chester branch . . . . . . . . . . . . . . . . . . . . (−) June 4, 1954
Ardmore branch . . . . . . . . . . . . . . . . . . . . . . . . (−) December 29, 1966

Miles of line . . . . . . . . . . . . . . . . . . . . . . . . . . . 51
Power system . . . . . . . . . . . . . . . . . . . . . . . . . . 600 v DC trolley
Passenger motor cars, 62½ in. gage, 1949 . . . . . 48
Vehicle series shown . . . . . . . . . . . . . . . . . . . . . 77 - 86
Length over all . . . . . . . . . . . . . . . . . . . . . . . . . . 49 ft. 2 in.
Weight in tons . . . . . . . . . . . . . . . . . . . . . . . . . . 21
Motors, quantity / builder / rating . . . . . . . . . . . 4 / GE-301B / 50 hp
Control, single or double end / type . . . . . . . . . . DE / GE - PCM
Approximate free speed . . . . . . . . . . . . . . . . . . . 45 mph
Builder / year delivered . . . . . . . . . . . . . . . . . . . Brill / 1932-1933

This group of cars was bought during the depth of the depression. With some belt-tightening measures, they helped Red Arrow lines (as the system was then known) cut costs and improve performance. They were a durable product despite light construction, serving about 50 years, the last few mainly as rush-hour trippers. Car 80 was acquired in 1982 by the Buckingham Valley Trolley Association.

PHILADELPHIA SURBURBAN TRANSPORTATION CO. 200 ► ►
Norristown High Speed Line

Philadelphia (69th St.) Villanova-Strafford . . . . . . . (+) May 22, 1907
Villanova-Norristown . . . . . . . . . . . . . . . . . . . . . . (+) August 26, 1912
Villanova-Strafford . . . . . . . . . . . . . . . . . . . . . . . (−) March 23, 1956

Miles of line (1943) . . . . . . . . . . . . . . . . . . . . . . . 18
Power system (1943) . . . . . . . . . . . . . . . . . . . . . . 730 v DC third rail
                                       (now changed to 650 v)
Passenger cars (1943) . . . . . . . . . . . . . . . . . . . . . 24
Vehicle series shown . . . . . . . . . . . . . . . . . . . . . . 200 - 209
Length over all . . . . . . . . . . . . . . . . . . . . . . . . . . 55 ft. 2 in.
Weight in tons . . . . . . . . . . . . . . . . . . . . . . . . . . 25
Motors, quantity / builder / rating . . . . . . . . . . . 4 / GE706B2 / 100 hp
Control, single or double end / type . . . . . . . . . . DE / GE PC C129
Approximate free speed . . . . . . . . . . . . . . . . . . . 70 mph (full field)
Builder / year delivered . . . . . . . . . . . . . . . . . . . Brill / 1931

When this design was undertaken by the then-Philadelphia & Western Railway, it was under the leadership of Dr. Thomas Conway, who had become noted for his work speeding up service on first the Chicago Aurora & Elgin R.R. and then the Cincinnati & Lake Erie.

Outstanding for their wind-tunnel-tested streamlined design, these cars amply justified their popular description as "bullets". They also stood the test of hard service over almost 60 years. Operated as one-man cars, they are capable of running in trains of up to three cars.

SEPTA, which took over PST, in early 1988 has retired them to weekend duty. Planned replacement is to be a high performance car with AC propulsion package, whose specifications were developed by MCERA Russell E. Jackson.

R. L. DAY / December 1949 / 69th Terminal, Upper Darby, PA

C. A. BROWN / April 10, 1943 / Conshohocken Road, PA

N. D. CLARK / March 1954 / Baltimore, MD

BALTIMORE & OHIO RAILROAD 10
Fells Point docks section
Canton district, Baltimore, MD

Docks area electrification . . . . . . . . . . . . . . . . . . . . . . (+) 1909    (−) 1954

| | |
|---|---|
| Miles of line . . . . . . . . . . . . . . . . . . . . . . . . . . . . . . . . | ±2 |
| Power system. . . . . . . . . . . . . . . . . . . . . . . . . . . . . . . . | 600 v DC trolley |
| Locomotives assigned . . . . . . . . . . . . . . . . . . . . . . . . | 1 |
| Vehicle series shown . . . . . . . . . . . . . . . . . . . . . . . . . | 10 |
| Length over all . . . . . . . . . . . . . . . . . . . . . . . . . . . . . . | 13 ft. |
| Weight in tons . . . . . . . . . . . . . . . . . . . . . . . . . . . . . . . | 10 |
| Motors, quantity / builder / type. . . . . . . . . . . . . . . . | 2 / GE / 58 |
| Builder / year delivered . . . . . . . . . . . . . . . . . . . . . . . | General Electric / 1909 |

The B&O had a little-known electrification in the docks area on the east side of Patapsco Bay approximately opposite its Camden station. It was fed from the conventional overhead trolley unlike the third rail powered Howard Street tunnel used by B&O main line trains.

This four-wheeler, reminiscent of a roundhouse "goat", is preserved at the wonderful B&O museum at Pratt and Poppleton Streets in Baltimore.

J. P. SHUMAN / January 22, 1950 / Linthicum Junction, MD

## BALTIMORE & ANNAPOLIS RAILROAD 18

| | |
|---|---|
| Annapolis-Camden station, Baltimore | (+) 1870s as steam RR. |
| Electrified at 6600 v 25 hz | (+) April 1908 |
| Re-electrified at 1200 v DC | (±) January 4, 1914 |
| Merged operation with Washington, Baltimore & Annapolis Electric R.R. and rerouted Shipley-Baltimore to WB&AERR Lombard/Howard terminal | (±) November 1, 1921 |
| Rerouted to B&O Camden station account remainder of WB&AE abandoned | (−) August 20, 1935 |
| Annapolis-Baltimore, rail passenger ended, freight dieselized | (−) February 5, 1950 |
| Diesel freight service since gradually cut back to Glenburnie | |

| | |
|---|---|
| Miles of line, 1950 | 27 |
| Power system | 1200 v DC catenary |
| Passenger motor cars, 1950 | 22 |
| Vehicle series shown | 18 |
| Length over all | 60 ft. (estimated) |

| | |
|---|---|
| Weight in tons | 59.5 |
| Motors, quantity / builder / rating | 4 / Wh 557W8 / 160 hp blown |
| Control, single or double end / type | DE / Wh HL 337D |
| Approximate free speed | 35 mph |
| Builder / year delivered | Jewett / 1909 |
| Rebuilt / year | Co. shops / 1914 et. seq. |

Originally, car 18 was 37, one of an order of three AC-powered baggage-passenger cars. It became box motor 300 when rewired for DC with force-ventilated motors and multi-notch control. MCERA Bill Ernst, later Master Mechanic of the Grand River Railway, served his apprenticeship on this job.

It was once more rebuilt, with a secondary floor covering steel rails and side sills added to increased weight on drivers, and hence, pulling power. To fit into WB&AE numbering, it then became 18. Until dieselization, it was B&A's only dedicated freight motive power.

In 1988, Baltimore's Mass Transit Administration has begun to build a modern light rail line from Dorsey (near Glen Burnie) through Baltimore to Hunts Valley, utilizing some of the old B&A and WB&AE alignments.

## LACKAWANNA & WYOMING VALLEY RAILROAD 403

| | |
|---|---|
| Scranton-Pittston, PA | (+) May 20, 1903 |
| Pittston-Hancock | (+) September 15, 1903 |
| Hancock-Wilkes Barre | (+) February 1, 1904 |
| Scranton tunnel bypass | (+) October 19, 1905 |
| Scranton-Dunmore branch | (−) October 25, 1945 |
| Remaining passenger service | (−) December 31, 1952 |
| Freight operations dieselized | (−) August 19, 1953 |
| Merged with Delaware Lackawanna & Western R.R., 1960 | |
| Only switching segments remained. | |

| | |
|---|---|
| Miles of line | 23 |
| Power system | 650 v DC trolley and overrunning 3rd rail |

| | |
|---|---|
| Motor cars owned at time of photo, passenger / locomotive | 22 / 3 |
| Vehicle series shown | 401-403 |
| Length over all | 32 ft. |
| Weight in tons | 53 |
| Motors, quantity / type / rating | 4 / Wh-557A8 / 140 hp |
| Control, single or double end / type | DE / Wh / HL |
| Approximate free speed | 33 mph |
| Builder / year delivered | L&WV shop / 1919 |

Amazingly, the cab and mechanical detail of Laurel Line's (L&WV) loco 403 were copied faithfully from 402, a Westinghouse AC prototype built in 1895 and re-equipped as a DC engine for sale to L&WV in 1906. Both were scrapped in 1956.

## NIAGARA JUNCTION RAILWAY 8

| | | |
|---|---|---|
| Switching trackage electrified | (+) 1913 (−) Nov. 1979 | Builder / year delivered ........................ Baldwin-Westinghouse / 1928 |

| | |
|---|---|
| Miles of line | 11 |
| Power system | 600 v DC catenary |
| Locomotives owned at peak | 16 |
| Vehicle series shown | 8 |
| Length over all | 37 ft. 6 in. |
| Weight in tons | 60 |
| Motors, quantity / builder / rating | 4 / Wh-308D5 / 140 hp |
| Control, single or double end / builder / type | DE / Wh - HLF 337D |
| Approximate free speed | 35 mph |

This railway was built to serve in the construction of hydro-electric generating stations. In 1948 it came under joint ownership of the New York Central, Erie and Lehigh Valley railroads, which became Conrail on April 1, 1976 and was changed to diesel power in 1979. Its chief importance has been in serving chemical plants 24 hours a day.

The locomotive shown was acquired, along with NJ 9, by Port Authority Transit at Lindenwold, NJ. As PATCo 405, it is used in work train movements. Three other NJ engines were acquired for switching service in Manhattan by Metro North and another has been preserved at Buffalo's Western New York Historical Society.

W. E. SCHRIBER / August 10, 1941 / Jamestown, NY

## JAMESTOWN WESTFIELD & NORTHWESTERN R.R. 304

| | |
|---|---|
| Jamestown-Mayville-Chautauqua, NY | (+) 1890 as steam R.R. |
| Mayville-Westfield | (↑) 1901 as steam R.R. |
| Jamestown-Westfield electrified | (+) August 20, 1914 |
| Street running in Jamestown | (−) March 31, 1940 |
| Jamestown-Westfield passenger service discontinued; freight dieselized | (−) 1947 |

| | |
|---|---|
| Miles of line | 32 |
| Power system | 600 v DC trolley |
| Passenger motor cars, 1941 | 5 |
| Vehicle series shown | 300 - 304 |
| Length over all | 53 ft. 6 in. |
| Weight in tons | 35 estimated |

| | |
|---|---|
| Motors, quantity / builder / rating | 4 / Wh 306A2 / 70 hp |
| Control, single or double end / type | SE / GE K35KK |
| Approximate free speed | 42 mph |
| Builder / year delivered | Cincinnati / 1914 |

This line made a direct across-the-platform transfer with the New York-Chicago main line of the New York Central System at Westfield. After a steep climb over the bluffs parallelling Lake Erie, the picturesque route followed Chautauqua Lake, often cutting through beachfront properties.

Passenger traffic, never very heavy, was originally stimulated by the Chautauqua Institution's meetings. By the late 1920s, it dwindled substantially and by the 1940s, there were rarely even a few dozen riders per day. JW&NW's relative longevity was due to early development of carload freight routed to/from Jamestown via the New York Central.

R. R. ANDREWS / 1951 / Port Colborne, ONT

E. VAN DUSEN / July 5, 1958 / Port Colborne, Ontario, Canada

◄ CANADIAN NATIONAL RAILWAYS
Niagara St. Catherines & Toronto Ry. 623

| | |
|---|---|
| Thorold-Pt. Colborne and several branches and extensions in stages | (+) 1879-1923 |
| Electrification begun | (+) 1887 |
| Passenger service, in stages | (−) 1931 - March 28, 1959 |
| Remaining trackage de-electrified by | (−) July 1960 |

| | |
|---|---|
| Miles of line | 63 |
| Power system | 600 v DC trolley |
| Motor cars owned as of 1927 passenger / freight / locomotive | 60 / 1 / 10 |
| Vehicle series shown | 620, 622, 623 |
| Length over all | 51 ft. 2 in. |
| Weight in tons | 31½ |
| Motors, quantity / builder / rating | 4 / Wh-548C2 / 100 hp |
| Control, single or double end / type | DE / Wh HL-15B2 |
| Approximate free speed | 55 mph |
| Builder / year delivered | Ottawa / 1930 |

The car shown here represents a mix of light and heavy weight technology and was among the last interurbans built in Canada. The series served first on the Windsor Essex & Lake Shore Railway, moving when WE&LS closed to the Montreal & Southern Counties Railway and shifting once again to NS&T after M&SC shut down.

LAKE ERIE & NORTHERN RAILWAY 955 ► ►
Canadian Pacific System

| | |
|---|---|
| Grand River Railway and predecessors Galt-Preston, Ontario, Canada | (+) July 26, 1894 |
| Galt-Hespeler | (+) January 1896 |
| Preston-Kitchener-Waterloo, in steps | (+) Aug. 1903 - Oct. 1904 |
| Lake Erie & Northern Railway Galt-Port Dover, in steps | (+) Feb. 1915 - July 1917 |
| Rerouted off city streets locally in Kitchener and in Galt | (±) 1921 |
| Rerouted locally in Preston | (±) November 8, 1937 |
| Waterloo-Kitchener passenger service | (−) April 24, 1938 |
| Kitchener-Galt-Pt. Dover passenger service | (−) April 23, 1955 |
| Remaining trackage de-electrified | (−) October 1, 1961 |

| | |
|---|---|
| Miles of line, Grand River Ry. | 51 |
| Lake Erie & Northern Ry. | 20 |
| Power system (incl. GRR since 1921) | 1500 v DC catenary |
| Motor cars (1950) Passenger / baggage-passenger / baggage | 16 / 4 / 1 |
| Vehicle series shown | 933 - 955 certain nos. |
| Length over all | 63 ft. 8½ in. |
| Weight in tons | 44 |
| Motors, quantity / builder / rating | 4 / Wh 545A6 / 75 hp |
| Control, single or double end / type | DE / Wh AB 334A3 |
| Approximate free speed | 48 mph |
| Builder / year built | Preston / 1915 |

◄ CANADIAN NATIONAL RAILWAYS
Niagara St. Catherines & Toronto Ry. 20

| | |
|---|---|
| Vehicle series shown | 20 |
| Length over all | 32 ft. 6 in. |
| Weight in tons | 55 |
| Motors, quantity / type / rating | 4 / GE-212 / 225 hp |
| Control, single or double end / builder | DE / GE |
| Builder / year delivered | General Electric / 1938 |
| Acquired from / date built | West Side Ry., Charleroi, PA ex. S. Brooklyn Ry. / 1914 |

An active short line freight carrier, NS&T had a variety of second-hand motive power of typical steeple-cab styles. Parent Canadian National passed engines and passenger cars between its various traction short line subsidiaries as their fortunes rose or fell. This motor was scrapped with the end of service in 1960.

The Lake Erie & Northern and Grand River railways were subsidiaries of the Canadian Pacific Railway and were fully integrated as to operation and management.

In the late 1940s and the 1950s the equipment and facilities underwent a vigorous modernization. A large part of this program was under the watchful eye of MCERA Bill Ernst, who, as Master Mechanic was instrumental in acquiring a couple of sturdy freight locomotives from the Salt Lake & Utah R.R. and in remotoring the steel passenger cars. Bill had learned his trade on the Baltimore-Annapolis line in the U.S.A.

F. J. GOLDSMITH, Jr. / May 16, 1954 / London, Ontario

## LONDON & PORT STANLEY RAILWAY Yard at London shops

London-Port Stanley, Ontario

| | |
|---|---|
| as a steam railway | (+) Oct. 2, 1856 |
| Electrified | (+) July 22, 1915 |
| Discontinued passenger service | (−) Feb. 2, 1957 |
| De-electrified | (−) 1963 |

| | |
|---|---|
| Miles of line | 24 |
| Power system | 1500 v DC catenary |
| Motor cars owned at time of photo, passenger / freight / locomotive | 10 / 1 / 3 |
| Vehicle series, typical motor car | 2 - 10 (even numbers) |
| Length over all | 61 ft. 2 in. |

| | |
|---|---|
| Weight in tons | 50 |
| Motors, quantity / builder / rating | 4 / GE-225B / 125 hp |
| Control, single or double end / type | DE / GE - M |
| Approximate free speed | 50 mph |
| Builder / year delivered | Jewett / 1915 |

In 1916 L&PS ordered cars 12 and 14 of the same general style as the 1915 cars described above but were ten feet longer. Third from the left in this view is one of four cars acquired from The Milwaukee Electric Lines and re-equipped for 1500 v. Next is 7, a coach built (but never delivered) to the St. Louis & Montesano, a project which failed to be completed. Barely visible at the extreme right is GE box cab locomotive L2.

49

J. P. SHUMAN / September 1958 / Port Huron, MI

## ST. CLAIR TUNNEL COMPANY 175
Grand Trunk Western Railway

| | | |
|---|---|---|
| Port Huron, MI-Sarnia, Ontario | . . . . . . . . . . . . . . | (+) May 17, 1908 |
| De-electrified, to diesels | . . . . . . . . . . . . . . . . . . . . . . . | (−) September 28, 1958 |

| | |
|---|---|
| Miles of line . . . . . . . . . . . . . . . . . . . . . . . . . . . . . . . . | 4 |
| Power system . . . . . . . . . . . . . . . . . . . . . . . . . . . . . . . . | 3300 v 25 hz catenary |
| Locomotives . . . . . . . . . . . . . . . . . . . . . . . . . . . . . . . . . | 10 |
| Vehicle series shown . . . . . . . . . . . . . . . . . . . . . | 175 - 176 |
| Length over all . . . . . . . . . . . . . . . . . . . . . . . . . . . . | 38 ft. |
| Weight in tons . . . . . . . . . . . . . . . . . . . . . . . . . . . . . | 72 |
| Motors, quantity / builder / rating . . . . . . . . . . . . . . . | 4 / Wh 151 / 180 hp |
| Control, single or double end / type . . . . . . . . . . . . . . | DE / Wh HB |

| | |
|---|---|
| Approximate free speed . . . . . . . . . . . . . . . . . . . . . . . . | 35 mph |
| Builder / year delivered . . . . . . . . . . . . . . . . . . . . . . . . | Baldwin-Westinghouse / 1916 |
| Acquired from / year . . . . . . . . . . . . . . . . . . . . . . . . . . . | CSS&SBRR / 1926 |

The very short electrification through the tunnel under the St. Clair River was one of the most cost-effective in the history of railroading, paying for itself many times over by overcoming the constraints of steam motive power on this vital and highly competitive international link.

The locomotive heading this freight was acquired when the change from 6600 v 25 hz to 1500 v DC made it surplus on the Chicago South Shore & South Bend Railroad.

E. VAN DUSEN / 1950 / Detroit, MI

## MICHIGAN CENTRAL RAILROAD 164
New York Central System

| | | |
|---|---|---|
| Detroit, MI-Windsor, ONT. tunnel | . . . . . . . . . . . | (+) 1910 |
| Detroit, MI-Windsor de-electrified | . . . . . . . . . . . | (−) December 29, 1953 |

| | | |
|---|---|---|
| Miles of line | . . . . . . . . . . . . . . . . . . . . . . . . . . . . . . | 5 |
| Power system | . . . . . . . . . . . . . . . . . . . . . . . . . . . . . . . | 600 v DC |
| | | underrunning third rail |
| Locomotives assigned | . . . . . . . . . . . . . . . . . . . . . . . . | 12 |
| Vehicle series shown | . . . . . . . . . . . . . . . . . . . . . . . . | 160 - 165 |
| Length over all | . . . . . . . . . . . . . . . . . . . . . . . . . . . . | 39 ft. 6 in. |
| Weight in tons | . . . . . . . . . . . . . . . . . . . . . . . . . . . . . | 120 |

| | | |
|---|---|---|
| Motors, quantity / builder / rating | . . . . . . . . . . . . . . . . | 4 / GE 209 / 300 hp |
| Control, single or double end / type | . . . . . . . . . . . . . . . | DE / GE / M |
| Approximate free speed | . . . . . . . . . . . . . . . . . . . . . . | 30 mph |
| Builder / year delivered | . . . . . . . . . . . . . . . . . . . . . . . | Alco - GE / 1910 |

This very short electrification connected Canada and the United States as did that of the Grand Trunk not many miles to the north.

The New York Central class R-1 locomotives built for this service were among the largest B°-B° steeple cab motors ever built and carried road numbers 7500-7505 when new. Dieselization and tunnel ventilation improvements obsoleted the electrification.

R. R. ANDREWS / Circa 1940 / Toledo, OH

TOLEDO EDISON COMPANY 1
Ryan power station

Miles of line . . . . . . . . . . . . . . . . . . . . . . . . . . . . . . . . . Approx. 1
Power system . . . . . . . . . . . . . . . . . . . . . . . . . . . . . . . . . 600 v DC trolley
Locomotives . . . . . . . . . . . . . . . . . . . . . . . . . . . . . . . . . . 5
Vehicle series shown . . . . . . . . . . . . . . . . . . . . . . . . . 1
Length over all . . . . . . . . . . . . . . . . . . . . . . . . . . . . . . . . 37 ft. 5 in.
Weight in tons . . . . . . . . . . . . . . . . . . . . . . . . . . . . . . . . 60
Motors, quantity / builder / rating . . . . . . . . . . . . . . . 4 / GE-257A / 170 hp

Control, single or double end / type . . . . . . . . . . . . . . . DE / GE M C90
Approximate free speed . . . . . . . . . . . . . . . . . . . . . . . 25 mph
Builder / year delivered . . . . . . . . . . . . . . . . . . . . . . . . General Electric / 1923

This installation is used for switching coal and materials. Its motive power includes the former CTA S-107 and S-108. It once connected with the Ohio Public Service Toledo-Port Clinton-Marblehead interurban and its successor, the Toledo & Eastern.

### TOLEDO & EASTERN RAILROAD 81 ▼

| | |
|---|---|
| Toledo-Pt. Clinton-Marblehead, OH . . . . . . . . . . . | (+) 1904-1906 in steps |
| Marblehead-Clay Center and west of Ryan<br>(via Toledo local transit company) also<br>all passenger service . . . . . . . . . . . . . . . . . . . . . . | (−) July 11, 1939 |
| Ryan-Clay Center . . . . . . . . . . . . . . . . . . . . . . . . . | (−) 1958 |

| | |
|---|---|
| Miles of line, 1955 . . . . . . . . . . . . . . . . . . . . . . . . . | 11 |
| Power system . . . . . . . . . . . . . . . . . . . . . . . . . . . . | 600 v DC trolley |
| Locomotives, 1955 . . . . . . . . . . . . . . . . . . . . . . . . | 2 |
| Vehicle series shown . . . . . . . . . . . . . . . . . . . . . . | 81 |
| Length over all . . . . . . . . . . . . . . . . . . . . . . . . . . . | 32 ft. |
| Weight in tons . . . . . . . . . . . . . . . . . . . . . . . . . . . | 60 |
| Motors, quantity / builder / type . . . . . . . . . . . . . | 4 / Wh 308 / 225 hp |
| Control, single or double end / type . . . . . . . . . . | DE / Wh-HL-337 |
| Approximate free speed . . . . . . . . . . . . . . . . . . . | 35 mph |
| Builder / year delivered . . . . . . . . . . . . . . . . . . . . | Baldwin-Wh / 1913 |
| Acquired from / year . . . . . . . . . . . . . . . . . . . . . . | International Ry. / 1950 |

   Opened under the name Toledo Port Clinton & Lakeside Railway, but operated most of its life as the Ohio Public Service Company, the short segment which survived longest was taken over by Toledo & Eastern, incorporated August 1945. It handled mainly dolomite quarried at Clay Center and coal to a Toledo Edison power plant at Ryan, in both cases through an interchange with the Wheeling & Lake Erie R.R. at Curtice, a midline point. As seen here, they did occasionally move a little other cargo.

### CLEVELAND UNION TERMINAL 215  ► ►
New York Central System

| | |
|---|---|
| Linndale-Collinwood via<br>Cleveland Union Terminal . . . . . . . . . . . . . . . . . . | (+) June 28, 1930 |
| De-electrified . . . . . . . . . . . . . . . . . . . . . . . . . . . | (−) 1953 |
| Partially dismantled . . . . . . . . . . . . . . . . . . . . . | (−) 1970s |

| | |
|---|---|
| Miles of line . . . . . . . . . . . . . . . . . . . . . . . . . . . . . | 17 |
| Power system . . . . . . . . . . . . . . . . . . . . . . . . . . . . | 3000 v DC catenary |
| Locomotives owned . . . . . . . . . . . . . . . . . . . . . . . | 22 |
| Vehicle series shown . . . . . . . . . . . . . . . . . . . . . . | 200 - 221, originally 1050 - 1071 |
| Length over all . . . . . . . . . . . . . . . . . . . . . . . . . . . | 80 ft. |
| Weight in tons . . . . . . . . . . . . . . . . . . . . . . . . . . . | 204 |
| Motors, quantity / builder / rating . . . . . . . . . . . . | 6 / GE-278C twin / 505 hp |
| Control, single or double end / type . . . . . . . . . . | DE / GE PCL |
| Approximate free speed . . . . . . . . . . . . . . . . . . . | 70 mph |
| Builder / year delivered . . . . . . . . . . . . . . . . . . . . | Alco - GE / 1930 |

   Main line through passenger trains of the New York Central and Nickel Plate railroads were zipped through the heart of the Cleveland metropolitan area by this facility.
   After diesels supplanted electrification, these powerful locomotives were rewired for 650 v third rail and saw many additional useful years on the NYC Hudson division into Grand Central Terminal, New York City.

G. KRAMBLES / June 1955/ Curtice, OH

G. KRAMBLES / September 9, 1951 / Cleveland Union Terminal, OH

W. C. JANSSEN / May 30, 1952 / Connellsville, PA

54

◄ WEST PENN RAILWAYS 832

Network of 62½" track gage rural lines connecting to the Pittsburgh, PA system at Trafford and McKeesport on the west and extending to link with Irwin, Greensburg, Latrobe, Herminie, Connellsville, Uniontown, Brownsville, Masontown and many small towns in the so-called "Coke Region" of western Pennsylvania. Built in steps from the 1890s to 1914, it was also abandoned in pieces from the late 1930s to 1952, with the last car leaving Connellsville for Uniontown at 11:30 p.m. on August 9.

| | |
|---|---|
| Miles of line (Coke Region peak) | 158 |
| Power system | 600 v DC trolley |
| Passenger motor cars, 1940 | 61 |
| Vehicle series shown | 831 - 842 |
| Length over all | 47 ft. 3 in. |
| Weight in tons | 16 |
| Motors, quantity / builder / rating | 4 / Wh 1425 / 35 hp |
| Control, single or double end / type | DE / W-K75A |
| Approximate free speed | 35 mph |
| Builder / year delivered | Cincinnati / 130 |

This system was notable in that its standard cars had no air brakes or other pneumatic devices, depending on dynamically-actuated tread and track brakes for retardation and hand-crank brake for holding. But the 831-class was an exception, having conventional trolley motors, control and air brakes. Built for use on the unconnected Allegheny Valley division, 832 served on the Connellsville-South Connellsville city route right through the last day and has been preserved at the Arden Trolley Museum.

MONONGAHELA WEST PENN PUBLIC SERVICE CO. 272 ▲
Parkersburg-Marietta division

| | |
|---|---|
| Parkersburg-Marietta interurban | (+) 1902 in steps |
| Marietta-Lowell-Beverly, OH | (+) 1908-1909 in steps |
| Merged with unconnected Fairmont-Clarksburg-Weston WV lines | (+) 1917 |
| Beverly-Marietta | (−) October 31, 1929 |
| Parkersburg-Marietta interurban | (−) April 12 / May 25, 1947 |

| | |
|---|---|
| Miles of line, 1940 system | 50 |
| Power system | 600 v DC trolley |
| Interurban motor cars at time of photo | Approx. 12 |
| Vehicle series shown | 268 - 274 even nos. |
| Length over all | 52 ft. 4 in. |
| Weight in tons | 29 |
| Motors, quantity / builder / rating | 4 / Wh-306CV / 60 hp |
| Control, single or double end / type | DE / Wh-HL |
| Approximate free speed | 40 mph |
| Builder / year delivered | Jewett / 1918 |

MWPPS operated the interstate division pictured here between Marietta, OH and Parkersburg, WV, and the unconnected network of city and interurban lines in the Fairmont-Clarksburg-Weston area. In 1943, after many years of development and integration into a regional power company, pursuant to the federal Securities and Exchange Act, the transit lines controlled by MWPPS were sold to a group called *City Lines of West Virginia*, which gave up rail operations altogether in just four more years.

H. STANGE / August 26, 1950 / New Duncan, SC

### PIEDMONT & NORTHERN RAILWAY 5612 ▲

| | |
|---|---|
| Anderson-Belton, SC | (+) 1907 (−) 1936 |
| Greenwood-Belton | (+) September 1911 |
| Charlotte-Gastonia, NC | (+) 1912 (−) psgr. Feb. 28, 1951 |
| Greenwood-Greenville, SC | (+) November 1912 |
| Greenwood-Spartanburg, SC | (+) March 3, 1914 |
| Greenwood-Spartanburg, SC | (−) Passenger, Oct. 31, 1951 |

Freight operation was dieselized, the final electric operation
being local switching in Charlotte which ended May 21, 1958.
Remains merged with Seaboard Coast Line, July 1, 1969.

| | |
|---|---|
| Miles of line | 180 |
| Power system | 1500 v DC catenary |
| Passenger cars / locos owned, 1950 | 14 / 23 |
| Vehicle series shown | 5612 |
| Length over all | 64 ft. 10 in. |
| Weight in tons | 126 |
| Motors, quantity / builder / rating | 8 / GE-212L / 300 hp |
| Control, single or double end / type | DE / Wh - HLF |
| Approximate free speed | 35 mph |
| Builder / year delivered | P&N shops / 1949 |

This railway, along with Illinois Terminal, pioneered in developing the 4-truck locomotive, starting with ordinary equipment from two typical motor cars worked into a double home-made frame. Ultimately, P&N had eight such "articulated" locos. Last built of these was 5612, which utilized some salvage from prototype 5600 plus a new propulsion package similar to then-recently built 5611. It became their most powerful electric engine, but was bumped by diesels and scrapped in 1954.

### PIEDMONT & NORTHERN RAILWAY 2102 ►

| | |
|---|---|
| Vehicle series shown | 2102 |
| Length over all | 74 ft. |
| Weight in tons | 42 |
| Motors, quantity / builder / rating | 8 / Wh- 557 / 175 hp |
| Control, single or double end / type | DE / Wh HL-15A |
| Approximate free speed | 55 mph |
| Builder / year delivered | Southern Car / 1914 |

Car 2102 was one of ten coach trailers (two of them with observation platforms) acquired during the railway's peak development period. In 1919 the straight coaches were motorized and one vestibule bulkhead was moved to form a small baggage compartment. In 1924 car 2102 was lengthened and strengthened to have a still larger baggage room. It saw service at one time or another on both the unconnected North and South Carolina divisions. In this view, the white building in the background is the old U.S. Mint.

G. G. McKINLEY / June 20, 1943 / New Albany, IN

## HOME TRANSIT INC. 200
Street car service, New Albany, IN

Took over from Indiana R.R. ................... (+) 1934
Discontinued street cars ...................... (−) December 29, 1945

Miles of line ........................... 6
Power system ......................... 600 v DC trolley
Motor cars ........................... 8 Birney single truck
　　　　　　　　　　　　　　　　　　　　　　　2 Cincinnati double truck
　　　　　　　　　　　　　　　　　　　　　　　1 Snow sweeper
Vehicle series shown ...................... 200
Length over all ......................... 28 ft. 3 in.
Weight in tons ......................... 14½
Motors, quantity ....................... 2 for traction
　　　　　　　　　　　　　　　　　　　　　　　1 for the brooms
Control, single or double end / type ............... DE / K

Approximate free speed ........................ 20 mph
Original number ............................... 300
Built for ........................................ Louisville & Sou. Ind. Tr. Co.
Builder / year delivered ........................ McGuire-Cummings / 1919
Acquired from / year .......................... Interstate P.S.Co. / 1934

New Albany is the westerly of the string of small cities on the Indiana side of the Ohio River opposite Louisville, Kentucky. Linked by a network of street car lines, its beginnings went back to horse-car days. At its peak, it was part of the Interstate Public Service system which extended from Louisville to Indianapolis, 117 miles to the north.

As railway operations of IPS shrank, a local group took over the then-remaining standard gage car lines in New Albany under the Name *Home Transit Inc.* and the 5 ft. gage line over the Ohio under the name *New Albany & Louisville Electric R.R., Inc.*

G. G. McKINLEY / August 1946 / Speeds, IN

## SOUTHERN INDIANA RY. Inc. 750

| | |
|---|---|
| Watson Jct.-Sellersburg, IN .................. | (+) 1907 |
| Built by Louisville & Northern Ry. & Ltg. (later part of Louisville-Indianapolis line operated by Indiana Railroad) | |
| Passenger service discontinued ............... | (−) November 1, 1939 |
| Acquired by Southern Indiana Ry. Inc. ......... | (±) March 18, 1940 |
| Changed to diesel operation ................... | (−) February 1947 |

| | |
|---|---|
| Miles of route ................................ | 5 |
| Power system................................. | 600 v DC trolley |
| Motor cars ................................... | 1 |
| Locomotives.................................. | 2 |
| Vehicle series shown ......................... | 750 |
| Length over all ............................... | 30 ft. 2 in. |
| Weight in tons ............................... | 54 |
| Motors, quantity / builder / rating ............ | 4 / Wh-333 / 125 hp |

| | |
|---|---|
| Control, single or double end / type............... | DE / Wh HL-337D |
| Approximate free speed ....................... | 35 mph |
| Built for / builder / year ....................... | Metropolitan St. Ry. / Co. shop / 1917 |
| Rebuilt for Interstate P.S. by / year ............ | AC&F / 1920 |
| Rebuilt for S.I.Ry. service .................... | Ind. RR / 1935, 1937, 1939 |

Connecting the Louisville Cement Company at Sellersburg to the Baltimore & Ohio R.R. at Watson Junction, this segment of the former Public Service Company of Indiana was saved to provide an alternative to the direct Pennsylvania R.R. connection to the plant.

This locomotive once served Kansas City Kaw Valley & Western R.R. as their 220, then Interstate Public Service (PSCI predecessor) as 605. Indiana Railroad renumbered it 750 and rebuilt it three times, adding weight, changing motors and control, and beefing up the air brake system. Ultimately, it was sold to American Aggregates Corporation at Greenville, OH, where it was converted to diesel and may still be working in 1988.

## CHICAGO SOUTH SHORE & SOUTH BEND R.R. 2

| | |
|---|---|
| Indiana Harbor-East Chicago, IN | (+) 1903 (−) July 27, 1926 |
| Tolleston Jct., Gary-Tolleston | (+) 1909 (−) 1910 |
| South Bend, IN-Pullman, IL, in steps | (+) June 1908 to July 1909 |
| Pullman-Randolph St., Chicago, trailers hualed by steam locos of Ill. Central R.R. | (+) 1912 (−) 1926 |
| Electrification changed from 6600 v 25 hz to 1500 v DC and extended Pullman-Randolph St., Chicago in steps | (+) July 13 to August 29, 1926 |
| East Chicago line relocation via Toll Road route | (+) September 15, 1956 |
| South Bend yard-Bendix | (−) July 7, 1970 |

| | |
|---|---|
| Miles of line | 90 |
| Power system | 1500 v DC catenary or trolley |
| Passenger cars at time of photo | 50 |
| Vehicle series shown | 1 - 9 |
| Length over all | 60 ft. |
| Weight in tons | 67 |
| Motors, quantity / builder / rating | 4 / Wh-567C11 / 210 hp |
| Control, single or double end / type | DE / Wh / HBF-XM160 |
| Approximate free speed | 72 mph |
| Builder / year delivered | Pullman / 1926 |

Although today's South Shore Line continues to pass the location shown here, West Tenth Street in Michigan City, practically everything in this scene is either gone or substantially changed. It does remain the grade crossing with the Amtrak Detroit-Chicago main line, but is now remotely controlled from Amtrak's Trail Creek tower about a mile away rather than the old frame building seen here.

E. VAN DUSEN / December 3, 1949 / Michigan City, IN

NORTHERN INDIANA PUBLIC SERVICE COMPANY 2 ▲

| | |
|---|---|
| Miles of line | ± 2 |
| Power system | 240 v storage battery and gas-electric generator |
| Vehicle series shown | 2 |
| Length over all | 52 ft. |
| Weight in tons | 118.5 |
| Motors, quantity / builder | 4 / GE 287 |
| Control, single or double end / builder | DE / GE dual power |
| Approximate free speed | 30 mph |
| Builder / year delivered | GE-Exide / 1940s |

This unit was built in 1926 as a demonstrator carrying builders' number 10035. After testing on the Chicago & North Western Railway in Chicago, it was sold in 1928 for use at the State Line Generating Station of Chicago's Commonwealth Edison.

Next assignment was at NIPSCo in Michigan City at the 60 hz generating station which had been built to replace the 25 hz plant originally developed by the Chicago Lake Shore & South Bend Railway. The power plant and the catenaries of the South Shore Line Lincoln yard are seen here, with CSS&SB's main line just out of range to the right. This loco wound up its days, it is believed, in an industrial plant.

## ◄ CHICAGO SOUTH SHORE & SOUTH BEND R.R. 702

| | |
|---|---|
| Locomotives owned at time of photo | 14 |
| Vehicle series shown | 701 - 707 |
| Length over all | 54 ft. |
| Weight in tons | 133 |
| Motors, quantity / builder / rating | 6 / GE-286 / 500 hp |
| Control, single or double end / type | DE / GE / PCL |
| Approximate free speed | 65 mph |
| Builder / year built | Alco - GE / 1930 |
| Acquired from / year | New York Central / 1954 |

One of the final production runs of electric locomotives for the New York Central System was the batch of 42 class R2 which saw duty in its New York and Detroit River services. South Shore Line rewired seven of them for 1500 v service from their original 650 v configuration, and modified the cabs to provide more crew space and better driving visibility. Doing this rebuilding work with its available in-house resources took from 1955 to 1968. But in only a few more years South Shore changed to diesel power for all its freight operations.

F. E. BUTTS / 1940 / Edgewater spur, Sheboygan, WI

F. E. BUTTS / January 28, 1940 / Watertown, WI

◄ WISCONSIN POWER & LIGHT COMPANY 1000

| | |
|---|---|
| Sheboygan-Sheboygan Falls | (+) 1899 |
| Sheboygan Falls-Plymouth | (+) 1904 |
| Plymouth-Elkhart Lake | (+) 1909 (−) 1927 |
| Sheboygan-Plymouth (except Edgewater power plant-C&NW spur) | (−) December 11, 1938 |
| Edgewater spur de-electrified | (−) 1941 |

| | |
|---|---|
| Miles of line | 23 |
| Power system | 600 v DC trolley |
| Locomotives owned | 1 |
| Vehicle series shown | 1000 |
| Length over all | 35 ft. 6 in. |
| Weight in tons | 50 |
| Motors, quantity / builder / rating | 4 / Wh 562-D5 / 100 hp |
| Control, single or double end / type | DE / Wh-HLF 337D2 |
| Approximate free speed | 35 mph |
| Builder / year delivered | Baldwin-Westinghouse / 1929 |

In an optimistic plan to develop interline interurban carload freight traffic with the connecting electric roads through Milwaukee to Chicago, WP&L acquired this one standard "B-1" steeple cab locomotive. As it turned out, it was the last piece of electric traction rolling stock operated by WP&L, keeping busy for a couple of years after the remainder of WP&L folded, switching coal from an interchange with the Chicago & North Western Railway to the Edgewater power plant at the south edge of Sheboygan. When replaced with a diesel, 1000 was sold to Bamberger Railroad (Salt Lake-Ogden, UT) and became their 551.

H. STANGE / June 10, 1951 / West Junction, Milwaukee, WI

◄ THE MILWAUKEE ELECTRIC RAILWAY & TRANSPORT CO. 1116
Milwaukee-Waukesha-Oconomowoc-Watertown line

| Segment | (in stages) | (in stages) |
|---|---|---|
| Milwaukee-Racine-Kenosha | (+) 1897 | (−) 1947 |
| Milwaukee-Waukesha | (+) 1898 | (−) 1951 |
| Waukesha-Watertown | (+) 1907-1908 | (−) 1940-1941 |
| Milwaukee-Hales Corners | (+) 1903 | (−) 1951 |
| Milwaukee-Port Washington | (+) 1907-1908 | (−) 1948 |
| Port Washington-Sheboygan | (+) 1908 | (−) 1945 |

| | |
|---|---|
| Miles of interurban line | 198 |
| Power system (1940) | 600 v DC trolley or catenary |
| Interurban passenger cars (1940) | Approx. 30 |
| Vehicle series shown | 1111 - 1119 |
| Length over all | 54 ft. 2½ in |
| Weight in tons | 48 |
| Motors, quantity / builder / rating | 4 / GE-254A / 140 hp |
| Control, single or double end / type | DE / GE M-C74A |
| Approximate free speed | 60 mph |
| Builder / year delivered | Kuhlman / 1909 |
| Rebuilder / year rebuilt | TM shops / 1926 |

A couple of days before abandonment (on February 1, 1940) car 1116 hosted a delegation of several CERA hardy. Here our motorman has brought the car around the tight loop behind the Watertown train shed and is ready for the 50-mile 85-minute trip to Milwaukee.

MILWAUKEE RAPID TRANSIT & SPEEDRAIL COMPANY ▲

| | |
|---|---|
| Milwaukee-Waukesha | (+) June 25, 1898 (−) June 30, 1951 |
| West Junction-Hales Corners | (+) June 27, 1903 (−) June 30, 1951 |

| | |
|---|---|
| Miles of line | 24 |
| Power system | 600 v DC overhead trolley |
| Vehicle series shown | 60 - 65 |
| Length over all | 42 ft. 6 in |
| Weight in tons | 19 |
| Motors, quantity / builder-type / rating | 4 / GE-247 / 40 hp |
| Control, single or double end / builder / type | SE / GE K-75E |
| Approximate free speed | 47 mph |
| Builder / year delivered | Cincinnati / 1928 |
| Acquired from / year delivered | Shaker Heights R.T. / 1949 |

A magnificent private right-of-way, free of grade crossings was built for the interurban lines of The Milwaukee Electric Railway & Light Company extending from the west edge of the central business district of Milwaukee to its west city limits. Its life was briefly prolonged from late 1949 by new owner Speedrail which introduced one-man trains. Here a short-turn car is shown crossing over to take the loop at West Junction.

G. KRAMBLES / May 1, 1960 / Highwood, IL

▲ ◀ CHICAGO NORTH SHORE & MILWAUKEE RAILROAD 300 and 738

| | |
|---|---|
| Evanston, IL-Milwaukee, WI, in steps . . . . . . . . . . | (+) 1895-1908 |
| Lake Bluff-Area (later Mundelein) IL . . . . . . . . . . . | (+) 1903-1905 |
| Extended Evanston-Chicago over Northwestern Elevated Railroad . . . . . . . . . . . . . | (+) August 6, 1919 |
| Howard St., Chicago-North Chicago Junction via Skokie Valley . . . . . . . . . . . . . . . . . . . . . . . . | (+) June 5, 1926 |
| Howard-Waukegan via Shore Line Route . . . . . . . . | (−) July 25, 1955 |
| All remaining service . . . . . . . . . . . . . . . . . . . . . . . | (−) January 20, 1963 |
| Howard St., Chicago-Dempster, Skokie Skokie Swift service by Chicago Transit Authority . . . . . . . . . . . . . . . . . . . . . . . . . . . . . . . | (+) April 20, 1964 |

| | | |
|---|---|---|
| Miles of line . . . . . . . . . . . . . . . . . . . . . | 122 | |
| Power system. . . . . . . . . . . . . . . . . . . . . . | 650 v DC trolley, catenary or overrunning 3rd rail | |
| Passenger motor cars, 1940 . . . . . . . . . . | 158 interurban, 34 city | |
| Vehicle series shown . . . . . . . . . . . . . . . | 300-302 | 737-751 |
| Length over all . . . . . . . . . . . . . . . . . . . . | 53 ft. 6 in | 55 ft. 3¼ in. |
| Weight in tons . . . . . . . . . . . . . . . . . . . . | 38½ | 52 |
| Motors, quantity / builder / rating . . . . . . . . | 4/GE-73c/75 | 4/Wh-557R5/145 hp |
| Control, single or double end / type . . . . . . . . | DE/GE-M-C6K | DE/Wh-HLF-28A |
| Approximate free speed . . . . . . . . . . . . . . | 50 mph | 77 mph |
| Builder / year delivered . . . . . . . . . . . . . . | Jewett/1909 | Pullman/1928 |

Before the Electroliners came in 1941, the extremes in age of operable passenger cars on the North Shore Line were the 300 (then under restoration by CERA) and the heavy Skokie Valley Route type, as marshalled here for a CERA inspection of the Highwood shops, followed by a ride in 300.

Shortly after Pearl Harbor day, CNS&M requested CERA relinquish car 300 for use as a temporary dressing room for wartime female shop workers. It was never actually so used, but survived to VJ day when it was vandalized in a celebration overflow from adjacent Fort Sheridan. Regrettably, CERA was not then in a position to take it on again. Its body became a diner in Libertyville and is now long since scrapped.

◀ ◀ CHICAGO NORTH SHORE & MILWAUKEE R.R. 803

| | |
|---|---|
| Vehicle series shown . . . . . . . . . . . . . . . . . . . . . . . . . | 801 - 804 |
| Length over all . . . . . . . . . . . . . . . . . . . . . . . . . . . . . . | 155 ft. 4 in. |
| Weight in tons . . . . . . . . . . . . . . . . . . . . . . . . . . . . . . | 107 |
| Motors, quantity / builder / rating . . . . . . . . . . . . . . . . . . | 8 / Wh-1443B1 / 100 hp |
| Double end control / builder / type . . . . . . . . . . . . . . | Wh - XMA-1 |
| Approximate free speed . . . . . . . . . . . . . . . . . . . . . . . | 75 mph |
| Builder / year delivered . . . . . . . . . . . . . . . . . . . . . . . | St. Louis / 1941 |

A grateful railroad took delivery of two articulated units like this just a few months before World War II broke out and stopped rail car production for four years. North Shore's only air-conditioned and streamlined equipment, each of these trains ran about 450 miles a day, year in and out except for a rare breakdown here and there with a general overhaul not even once a year. This set a fantastic industry-wide record.

After CNS&M operation ended in 1963, these trains were acquired by Red Arrow Lines where they made rush-hour trippers on the 14-mile Norristown-69th Street (Upper Darby, PA) run.

Locomotives (1946) . . . . . . . . . . . . . . . . . . . . . . . 10
Vehicle series shown . . . . . . . . . . . . . . . . . . . . . . . 455 - 456
Length over all . . . . . . . . . . . . . . . . . . . . . . . . . . . 40 ft.
Weight in tons . . . . . . . . . . . . . . . . . . . . . . . . . . . 70
Motors, quantity / builder / rating . . . . . . . . . . . . . 4 / GE-251 / 200 hp
Control, single or double end / builder / type . . . . . . . . DE / GE / M
Approximate free speed . . . . . . . . . . . . . . . . . . . . 40 mph
Builder / year delivered . . . . . . . . . . . . . . . . . . . . . General Electric / 1927

To serve industries on unwired track, such as in its Niles Center (now Skokie) Weber Industrial District, North Shore Line purchased two dual power (battery-trolley) locos like this. In addition to being able to run in the usual way from the 650 v trolley, they had 195 2-volt Exide battery cells rated 600 ampere-hours. Theoretically, one of these motors could haul 33 loaded freight cars a distance of 5 miles at a speed of 20 mph, then get back on wire, charge up an hour or so and do it again!

C&NWRy-CECo Northwest Station . . . . . . . . . . . . (+)1912  (−) 1970s

Miles of line . . . . . . . . . . . . . . . . . . . . . . . . . . . . 1
Power system . . . . . . . . . . . . . . . . . . . . . . . . . . . . . 500 v DC underrunning
                                                                     third rail
Locomotives at time of photo . . . . . . . . . . . . . . . . . 4
Vehicle series shown . . . . . . . . . . . . . . . . . . . . . . . S-1 to S-4
Length over all . . . . . . . . . . . . . . . . . . . . . . . . . . . 33 ft. 2 in.
Weight in tons . . . . . . . . . . . . . . . . . . . . . . . . . . . 60
Motors, quantity / builder / rating . . . . . . . . . . . . . 4 / GE-207 / 125
Control, single or double end / type . . . . . . . . . . . . . . DE / GE / M
Approximate free speed . . . . . . . . . . . . . . . . . . . . . 16 mph
Builder / year delivered . . . . . . . . . . . . . . . . . . . . . General Electric / 1912

This unique electrification linked a then-new Northwest Generating Station to the Chicago & North Western's Wisconsin Division and to docks along the north branch of the Chicago River to bring coal and other supplies. It succumbed to obsolescence from modern generation technology. In this view the motorman is making a run for it to coast over California avenue where there was obviously no source of electricity. This engine is preserved by Illinois Railway Museum.

G. KRAMBLES / April 1951 / California & Addison, Chicago

T. H. DESNOYERS (G. KRAMBLES) / September 1955 / Western at Van Buren

CHICAGO TRANSIT AUTHORITY ▲
Temporary route of Garfield service

Street level operation to permit demolition of elevated railroad structure and excavation of an open cut subway in the median of a new Congress (now Eisenhower) freeway

| | |
|---|---|
| In service | (+) September 20, 1953 |
| Replaced by new fully grade-separated route | (−) June 22, 1958 |

| | |
|---|---|
| Miles of line | 10 |
| Power system | 630 v DC third rail |
| Motor cars assigned to Garfield service | 103 |
| Rapid transit vehicle series shown | 4129 - 4250 |
| Length over all | 48 ft. 6 in. |
| Weight in tons | 35 |
| Motors, quantity / builder / rating | 2 / GE-243 / 170 hp |
| Control, single or double end / type | DE / Wh / ABLFM-C36 |
| Approximate free speed | 42 mph |
| Builder / year delivered | Cincinnati / 1915-1916 |

Here a northbound Western Avenue PCC car is waiting for the westbound Garfield rapid transit train. All vehicles proceeded on traffic signals, which were timed to permit one train to proceed every alternate 60-second cycle. Despite this difficult operation (with live third rail) there were no serious accidents. Absence of intermediate stations in the construction zone, plus closure of several others along the route saved about as much trip time as was added by the street running in the 2½ mile shoo-fly.

CHICAGO TRANSIT AUTHORITY 2819 ► ►
Temporary route of Garfield service

| | |
|---|---|
| Vehicle series shown | 2813 - 2857 |
| Length over all | 47 ft. 4¼ in. |
| Weight in tons | 34½ |
| Motors, quantity / builder / rating | 2 / Wh-114 / 170 hp |
| Control, single or double end / type | DE / Wh-AB-11 |
| Approximate free speed | 40 mph |
| Builder / year delivered | AC&F / 1904 |

Chicago's rapid transit system began as four independent operating companies each with their own distinctive features of car design. Here is seen Metropolitan West Side Elevated Railway's second style of motor car, with monitor roof, boxy body and steel reinforced underframe having exposed side sill beams. Cars of this type last saw service in 1957.

◄ CHICAGO TRANSIT AUTHORITY 1260
Evanston service

| | |
|---|---|
| Howard station-Central St., Evanston .......... | (+) May 16, 1908 |
| Central-Linden Ave., Wilmette ............... | (+) April 2, 1912 |

| | |
|---|---|
| Miles of line, Evanston branch .................... | 4 |
| Power system, 1952 .......................... | 630 v DC trolley or overrunning third rail |
| Vehicle series shown ........................ | 1260 - 1269 |
| Length over all ............................. | 47 ft. 1 in. |
| Weight in tons ............................. | 21½ |
| Motors, quantity / builder / rating ............... | none |
| Control, single or double end / type............. | DE / Wh-ALM - C36 |
| Builder / year delivered ...................... | AC&F / 1907 |

Forty trail coaches were delivered to the Northwestern Elevated Railroad by the Ohio Falls plant of American Car & Foundry Company at Jeffersonville, IN. The care given to appearance was accentuated in the original paint job by elaborate striping and the cars included some innovations in technology such as air-operated sliding doors and transverse seats. In 1914 twenty were motorized and in 1916 another ten like 1260 were equipped as driving (control) trailers. In 1950 seven more were motorized. Car 1268 is preserved currently at Illinois Railway Museum.

Because of surface grade operation the Evanston line was once mostly powered through overhead trolley, but in recent years it has been changed to run entirely from third rail.

▼ CHICAGO TRANSIT AUTHORITY 251-type and 6201-type
Howard Service, North-South Route
North portion (Howard Street-Downtown)

| | |
|---|---|
| Wilson-Loop via elevated ............. | (+) May 31, 1900 |
| Wilson-Central, Evanston via Chgo Milw & St. Paul RR r-o-w ........... | (+) May 16, 1908 |
| Rerouted some service Armitage-Downtown via State St. subway ..... | (±) October 17, 1943 |
| Rerouted remaining service via subway and began AB service ....... | (±) July 31, 1949 |

| | | |
|---|---|---|
| Miles of line .......................... | approx. 10 | |
| Power system.......................... | 630 v DC 3rd rail | |
| Cars assigned, 1957 .................. | 480 | |
| Vehicle series shown ................. | 251 - 320 | 6201 - 6470 |
| Length over end sills ................. | 46 ft. 8½ in. | 48 ft. |
| Weight in tons ....................... | 29½ | 20½ |
| Motors, quantity / type / rating ....... | 2/Wh121/85 hp | 4/Wh1432LK/55 hp |
| Control, single or double end / type ........ | DE / WhAL(b) | SE / Wh PCC |
| Approximate free speed ................ | 35 mph | 50 mph |
| Builder / year delivered ............... | Jewett / 1905 | St. Louis / 1954 |

The Jewett-built "gate" cars were on a CERA inspection trip, nearing their final days of service when this scene was recorded to contrast them with the new PCC cars. The old cars had an unusual control system where the master controller energized the train line wires with 3rd rail voltage and this, through relays in the #1 end cab, commanded the 12-volt battery operated Westinghouse type 251 switch groups. The complexity was required to work in trains with line powered Sprague control cars.

R. N. LUKIN / April 14, 1957 / Jarvis station, Chicago, IL

## CHICAGO TRANSIT AUTHORITY 4445-4446
Garfield service

| | |
|---|---|
| Loop-Laramie Ave. | (+) June 1895 - Oct. 1904 in steps |
| Laramie-Des Plaines, Forest Park via Aurora, Elgin & Chicago Ry | (+) March 11, 1905 |
| Desplaines-Roosevelt, Westchester via Chicago, Aurora & Elgin RR | (+) Oct. 1, 1926   (−) Dec. 9, 1951 |
| Roosevelt-22nd & Mannheim | (+) Dec. 1, 1930   (−) Dec. 9, 1951 |
| Rerouted Halsted-Sacramento via Van Buren surface tracks | (±) September 20/27, 1953 |
| Rerouted via Dearborn subway and median of Congress Expressway, service extended to Logan Sq., name changed to Congress branch West-Northwest route | (±) June 22, 1958 - March 20, 1960 |
| Extended Logan Sq-Jefferson Park | (+) February 1, 1970 |
| Extended Jefferson Park-O'Hare | (+) 1983-1984 in two steps |

| | |
|---|---|
| Vehicle series shown | 4406 - 4455 |
| Length over all | 48 ft. 6 in. |
| Weight in tons | 38½ |
| Motors, quantity / builder / rating | 2 / Wh-567 / 170 hp |
| Control, single or double end / type | SE / Wh-ABLFM-XM110 |
| Approximate free speed | 45 mph |
| Builder / year delivered | Cincinnati / 1925 |

Chicago's 4000s were built as double-end cars, but the #2 end cabs were deactivated to reduce the cost and completion time for the installation of remote door control, an early project after CTA takeover. The job paid back its cost in about 9 months through reducing crew needed for door operation to one man per train. It previously required, in addition to the motorman, one man for every two cars of a steel train or one per car on most wood trains.

In this view the L structure is temporarily supported out of the way of construction of the expressway in which today's replacement service operates.

## CHICAGO TRANSIT AUTHORITY 2009 ▶

Condensed chronology of Lake service

| | |
|---|---|
| State St.-Laramie Ave. | (+) 1893-1894 in steps |
| Electrified | (+) 1895 |
| Laramie-Marengo, Forest Pk. | (+) 1899-1910 in steps |
| Lake-Madison via Market | (−) April 4, 1948 |
| Laramie-Marengo rerouted via C&NWRy elevation | (±) October 28, 1962 |
| Loop-95th/Dan Ryan | (+) September 28, 1969 |

| | |
|---|---|
| Miles of line | 10 (Harlem - #12 tower, Loop) |
| Power system | 630 v DC overrunning 3rd rail; except trolley Central-Harlem to Oct. 1962 |
| Motor cars assigned | 140 (1964) |
| Vehicle series shown | 2001 - 2180 |
| Length over all | 48 ft. 6 in. |
| Weight in tons | 24 |
| Motors, quantity / builder / rating | 4 / GE-1250K1 / 100 hp |
| Control, single or double end / type | SE / GE SCM |
| Approximate free speed | 52-55 mph (governed) |
| Builder / year delivered | Pullman / 1964 |

Chicago's many rapid transit branches, although developed by several competitors, by fortuitous decision adopted a commonality of car design that permitted any car to run over any line of any of the underlying companies. This trait, not shared by any other mature metro system in the western world, resulted in incremental evolution of technical features.

Starting with the original wood cars of 1890-1910, the next major breakthrough came with the heavy steels of 1914-1924, progressed through the aluminum-sheathed, all-electric PCC fleet of 1947-1960 into the high-performance fleet of 1964 to date. This current group, beginning with the type shown, represented significant advances in appearance and passenger comfort as well as performance.

W. C. JANSSEN / September 19, 1953 / Hannah, Oak Park, IL

◄ ◄ CHICAGO TRANSIT AUTHORITY 6131-6132

| Chronology of Ravenswood service | |
|---|---|
| Loop-Clark Jct. | (+) May 31, 1900 |
| Clark Jct.-Western | (+) May 18, 1907 |
| Western-Kimball | (+) December 14, 1907 |

| | |
|---|---|
| Miles of line | 11 (Kimball-Loop) |
| Power system | 630 v DC third rail |
| Motor cars assigned, 1951 | 165 |
| Vehicle series shown | 6131 - 6200 |
| Length over all | 48 ft. 6 in. |
| Weight in tons | 21 |
| Motors, quantity / builder / rating | 4 / Wh 1432LK / 55 hp |
| Control, single or double end / builder / type | SE / Wh / XDA1A PCC |
| Approximate free speed | 50 mph |
| Builder / year delivered | St. Louis / 1951 |

By the time of this photo, CTA was well into a 774-car commitment to the PCC all-electric vehicle, a technology that became unique to CTA among the heavy rapid transit lines of the world. Many of the bugs of this radical adaptation of the PCC concept were worked out in the Ravenswood experience of the early 1950s as problems appeared that would never occur in PCCs applied to street railway service.

▲ CHICAGO AURORA & ELGIN RAILWAY (third rail div'n) 428

Operations began August 25, 1902 between Laramie station, on the west side of Chicago, and Aurora. By 1910, lines had been extended to Batavia, Elgin, Geneva-St. Charles and into downtown Chicago. A branch to Mount Carmel was replaced 1926-1930 by a Westchester branch (operated by Chicago Rapid Transit) but it was abandoned in 1951. The St. Charles branch ended in 1937, and through service into Chicago was cut back to Desplaines station in 1953.

| | |
|---|---|
| All remaining passenger service | (−) July 3, 1957 |
| All remaining freight service | (−) June 10, 1961 |

| | |
|---|---|
| Miles of line, 1953 | 54 |
| Power system | 600 v DC trolley and overrunning 3rd rail |
| Motor cars, 1953 | Approx. 62 |
| Vehicle series shown | 420 - 434 |
| Length over all | 55 ft. 3¼ in. |
| Weight in tons | 55 |
| Motors, quantity / builder / rating | 4 / GE-254 / 145 hp |
| Control, single or double end / type | DE / GE-M C-165A |
| Approximate free speed | 75 mph |
| Builder / year delivered | Cincinnati / 1927 |

Westbound PM-rush-hour CA&E limited, with cars for both Aurora and Elgin, awaits lineup at home signal controlling grade crossing with Soo Line and Chicago Great Western (on B&OCT) railroads. One day later CA&E service was cut back to Desplaines station, just west of here, to make way for construction of today's Interstate 290. Note two CTA rapid transit trains, delayed en route to allow the interurban to run around them, following closely, on "sight," without signal protection.

W. C. JANSSEN / November 8, 1952 / Carlinville, IL

## ILLINOIS TERMINAL RAILROAD SYSTEM 1593 ▲

Peoria-Springfield-St. Louis and
  branch lines, in steps ......................... (+) 1904-1910 (−) 1953-1958
Peoria-Bloomington-Decatur, in steps .......... (+) 1905-1907 (−) 1953
Danville-Urbana/Champaign-Decatur-
  Springfield and branches, in steps ........... (+) 1899-1904 (−) 1928-1953

Miles of line ........................................ 400
Power system ....................................... 600 v DC trolley or catenary
Locomotives owned, 1945 ........................ 46
Vehicle series shown .............................. 1579 - 1598
Length over all ..................................... 52 ft. 5 in.
Weight in tons ...................................... 80

Motors, quantity / builder / rating ................ 8 / GE-205B blown / 125 hp
                                     (for locomotive shown)
Control, single or double end / type ................ DE / GE-M C6
Approximate free speed ........................... 35 mph
Builder / year delivered ........................... Decatur shop / 1924-1928

Adaptive re-use of trucks, control and motors salvaged from retired passenger cars, plus ingenious application of the carbody design of its older, two-truck (Class B) locomotive yielded Illinois Terminal the class C workhorse for its 1920-1930 period of freight traffic expansion.

The distinctive gothic architecture of ITS passenger cars, developed when J. M. Bosenbury was Superintendent of Motive Power, brought a family resemblance to these freight engines.

W. C. JANSSEN / November 9, 1952 / Hamel, IL

W. C. JANSSEN / September 11, 1955 / Springfield belt, IL

| Vehicle series shown | 273 - 285 |
|---|---|
| Length over all | 57 ft. |
| Weight in tons | 53½ |
| Motors, quantity / builder / rating | 4 / GE-222 / 140 hp |
| Control, single or double end / type | DE / GE-M |
| Approximate free speed | 65 mph |
| Builder / year delivered | St. Louis / 1913 |

Here's train 89 en route Decatur-St. Louis dashing non-stop through the hamlet of Hamel (!), criss-crossing highway US-66 southbound in the prairie country just north of Edwardsville.

When ITRR introduced streamlined trains in January 1949 it included one daily round trip Decatur-St. Louis of a two-car set, operating as train 91 south and 94 north, carrying the name "City of Decatur". In September 1950 this equipment was re-assigned to Peoria-St. Louis service with the train name "Sangamon". The direct Decatur-St. Louis service was continued, but using a standard old-type air-conditioned car.

| Main line interurban motor cars, 1955 | Approximately 20 | | |
|---|---|---|---|
| Vehicle series shown | 300-302 | 330-331 | 350-352 |
| Length over all | 66 ft. 10 in. | 65 ft. 4 in. | 65 ft. 4 in. |
| Weight in tons | 55 | 50½ | 54 |
| Motors, quantity / type (100 hp each) | 4 | 2 | 4 |
| | GE1240A2 | GE1240A2 | GE1240A2 |
| Control, single or double end / type | SE/GE-PCM | -/GE-PCM | -/GE-PCM |
| Approximate free speed at 600 v | 60 mph | 60 mph | 60 mph |
| Builder / year delivered | St. Louis Car Co. / October 1949 | | |

These trains represent Illinois Terminal's effort to modernize Peoria- and Decatur-St. Louis services that turned into a string of disappointments in judgment and technology. Coupled 300s could not negotiate sharp curves in the St. Louis, Springfield and Peoria terminals. Three-car trains needed more power than always available so that acceleration and speed were less than for the cars replaced.

The diner-lounge cars drew few riders even with reasonably priced meals and small seat charge instead of first class fares. After its trainmen's union forced addition of a brakeman to the crew, IT took off the 350s, saving the cost of the non-union porter.

Despite all this, a full train of IT streamliners was a thrilling sight as it rolled across the viaduct spanning the Gulf Mobile & Ohio and Illinois Central railroads on the belt line around Springfield.

## TORSIONAL RIGIDITY — AN IMPORTANT FACTOR IN VEHICLE SUSPENSION DESIGN

The prevailing widespread use of articulated cars fostered by the need to operate large units over mostly existing streetcar lines will in due course be superseded by long single vehicles as evolved for rapid transit lines. With these, mostly air-sprung, vehicles the torsional characteristics will have to be considered with particular reference to the magnitude of possible wheel load reduction likely to be encountered on "twisted" track and the resultant propensity to derailment.

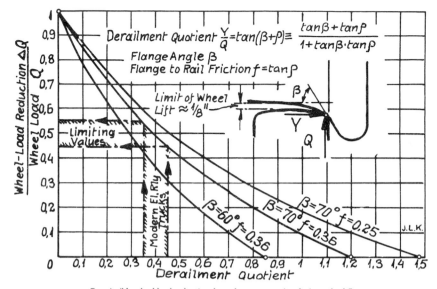

Permissible wheel load reduction depends on suspension design, wheel flange angle and flange-to-rail friction. Flange lubrication reduces wear and danger of rail climbing by facilitating the wheel slipping back onto the rail. With most modern truck designs wheel unloading should not exceed 0.5 of static load but up to 0.6 can be permitted with certain axle guiding solutions.

The relevant problems became acute shortly before World War II with the derailment of a number of electric locomotives and torsionally rigid wagons when leaving superelevated curves and also at low speeds when running over frost-distorted straight track. The problem was accentuated by torsionally rigid bodywork combined with relatively stiff suspensions.

More recent examination and evaluation of track records relating to some 7000 miles of track of five European railways revealed that generally track twists of 1 in 150 or 0.666% had to be considered while the ratio of wheel load reduction (delta Q) to static wheel load Q should not exceed 0.6. This could not be readily met by many existing wagons some of which derailed over track twists below 0.4%. The manager of a major oil company operating a large tanker fleet said, "From the time of this first derailment the dreaded expression *delta Q over Q* or, as we refer to it *delta Q over Koffman*, became a nightmare." resolved by careful attention to suspension design.

Further tests and evaluation led to an agreement among leading European state railways for the anticipated track twist to relate to truck wheel base and the distance between truck centers. The acceptable reduction of the wheel load was to be related to the flange angle and the suspension design. To be on the safe side, the flange-to-rail friction was based on test results, taken at 0.36. With modern positively-located wheelsets the wheel load reduction should not exceed 0.5 although up to 0.6 was allowed with some earlier designs to facilitate accommodation in curves, permitting a wheel that may start to climb a rail to drop back onto it.

The relevant torsional rigidity determinations can be carried but with the aid of hydraulic jacks and load measuring cells. Designers should assess prevailing track conditions and specify limiting overall vehicle twist rigidity values to safeguard reliable operation particularly when it comes to pneumatic suspensions. With these suspensions possible failure and the need to run on the emergency springs could result in a torsionally rigid, derailment-prone vehicle.

J.L.K.

C. A. BROWN / 1950 / Granite City, IL.

## ILLINOIS TERMINAL RAILROAD SYSTEM 123
St. Louis-Alton division

| | |
|---|---|
| Alton-St. Louis via E. St. Louis | (+) 1904 |
| Rerouted via McKinley Bridge | (±) 1933 |
| Alton-St. Louis | (−) March 7, 1953 |
| Miles of this route | 26 |
| Power system | 600 v DC trolley/catenary |
| Passenger motor cars assigned, 1950 | 9 |
| Vehicle series shown | 120 - 123 |
| Length over all | 53 ft. 8 in. |
| Weight in tons | 29.5 |
| Motors, quantity / builder / rating | 4 / GE-205B / 100 hp |
| Control, single or double end / type | DE / GE M C6K |

| | |
|---|---|
| Approximate free speed | 50 mph |
| Builder / year delivered | E. St. Louis & Sub'n / 1922-1924 |
| Acquired from / year | ESL&S / June 1930 |

This type of car was built for suburban service on the E. St. Louis & Suburban Railway's Lebanon line. It had Brill trucks, K35 control and 50 hp motors. IT added couplers, steel pilots and the equipment listed, using salvage from retired 350-class.

The 120s could run in multiple, but not with similar appearing 100-104. The 100s were substantially faster, able to make the 26-mile run as a limited in 45 minutes, despite street running in Granite City and slow going over McKinley Bridge and into St. Louis.

G. KRAMBLES / February 22, 1954 / Baden station, St. Louis, MO

## ST. LOUIS WATERWORKS RAILWAY 10
Grand Avenue-Baden-Chain of Rocks, Missouri
with passenger service Baden-Chain of Rocks

(+) January 8, 1902
(−) April 30, 1955

| | |
|---|---|
| Miles of line | 7¾ |
| Power system | 600 v DC trolley |
| Motor cars owned, passenger / service | 4 / 1 |
| Vehicle series shown | 10 - 11 |
| Length over all | 39 ft. |
| Weight in tons | 25 (estimated) |
| Motors | 4 |
| Control, single or double end / type | DE / K35 |

| | |
|---|---|
| Approximate free speed | 35 mph |
| Builder / year delivered | St. Louis / 1914 |

This unusual railway was used to move employees between residential areas (and a street car connection) near the north city limits of St. Louis to what was then a remote pumping station for the growing city's water supply. It also handled occasional cars of chemicals and equipment from an interchange with the Chicago Burlington & Quincy Railroad.

As nearby land began to develop, it began to operate as a common carrier with hourly trips and a 5 cent fare, but was ultimately replaced with bus and truck operations by others. Car 10 was donated in 1958 to the National Museum of Transport in St. Louis.

## ST. LOUIS CAR COMPANY 11

| | |
|---|---|
| Yard of carbuilding plant | (+) 1899    (−) 1973 |
| Miles of line | ± 2 |
| Power system | 600 v trolley |
| Vehicle series shown | 9, 11 |
| Length over all | 34 ft. |
| Weight in tons | 60 |
| Motors, quantity / builder / rating | 4 / GE-69 / 200 hp |
| Control, single or double end / type | DE / GE-M |
| Approximate free speed | 35 mph |

| | |
|---|---|
| Builder / year | Illinois Traction / 1914 |
| Acquired from / year | Ill. Term. R.R. / 1959 |

This locomotive was one of 18 built over an eight year span starting in 1910, to a home-crafted design, for service on the 400-mile ITS network. After more than 40 years of such duties, it was sold for switching at the car-builder's plant at 8000 N. Broadway in St. Louis. It shared this assignment with locos 7 (ex-Indiana R.R.) and 9 (another ex ITS class B, 1567). They replaced 50-year old wood frame, cab-on-a-raft home-built engines.

R. V. MEHLENBECK / May 28, 1939 / 4th Ave. & 3rd St. SE, Cedar Rapids, IA

### CEDAR RAPIDS & IOWA CITY RAILWAY 116

| | |
|---|---|
| Vehicle series shown | 110, 111, 116-119 |
| Length over end sills | 44 ft. 3 in. |
| Weight in tons | 24 |
| Motors, quantity / builder / rating | 4 / GE-706A / 100 hp |
| Control, single or double end / type | SE / GE-PC10 C129 |
| Approximate free speed | 70 mph (full field) |
| Builder / year delivered | Cincinnati / 1930 |
| Acquired from / year | Cincinnati & Lake Erie / 1939 |

John Munson, master mechanic of the Crandic line, knew a bargain when he saw one, acquiring six of the high speed coaches of the Cincinnati & Lake Erie Railroad while it was still preparing to run its last interurban passenger train on May 13, 1939. A good friend to CERA, Crandic agreed to a trial of the first C&LE car to arrive and here's that trip, put together on understandably short notice when 116's anticipated arrival in Iowa could be confirmed. After a quick inspection and wash job, car 116, still in its C&LE livery and with Munson at the controls, made her first 50 miles on Crandic celebrating CERA's first anniversary. A bittersweet coincidence was the finale of C&LE freight switching (Cumminsville-Mt. Healthy, OH) three days later.

The 116 is preserved at Branford Trolley Museum.

C. A. BROWN / May 7, 1944 / Iowa City, IA

E. VAN DUSEN / July 18, 1953 / Denver, IA

◄ CEDAR RAPIDS & IOWA CITY RAILWAY 120

| | |
|---|---|
| Cedar Rapids-Iowa City, IA | (+) August 13, 1904 |
| Cedar Rapids-Mt. Vernon | (+) March 14, 1914 |
| Mount Vernon-Lisbon | (+) 1914 |
| Cedar Rapids-Lisbon | (−) July 27, 1928 |
| Cedar Rapids-Iowa City passenger | (−) May 30, 1953 |
| Freight service dieselized | (−) 1953 |

| | |
|---|---|
| Miles of line, 1950 | 27 |
| Power system | 600 v DC trolley |
| Passenger cars, 1950 | 7 |
| Vehicle series shown | 120 |
| Length over all | 46 ft. |
| Weight in tons | 26 |
| Motors, quantity / builder / rating | 4 / GE-706 / 100 hp |
| Control, single or double end / type | DE / Wh HL-15B3 |
| Approximate free speed | 65 mph (full field) |
| Builder / year delivered | Pullman / 1931 |
| Acquired from / year | Indiana RR / July 1942 |

Circling the loop at the University of Iowa campus in Iowa City. Built as #65, one of Indiana Railroad's 35 light weight high speed cars, 120 became the last surviving serviceable car on IR's Indianapolis-Seymour franchise run. Although built as a one-man car and used that way in Indiana, Crandic always operated it with a two man crew. Today, restored to IR configuration, it is at the Illinois Railway Museum.

◄ WATERLOO CEDAR FALLS & NORTHERN RAILWAY 100

| | |
|---|---|
| Waterloo-Cedar Falls | (+) June 9, 1897 |
| Waterloo-Denver, IA | (+) December 31, 1901 |
| Denver-Waverly | (+) December 29, 1910 |
| Waterloo-Cedar Rapids | (+) 1912-Sept. 14, 1914 |
| Waterloo-Waverly passenger | (−) August 1955 |
| Waterloo-Cedar Rapids passenger | (−) February 20, 1956 |
| Waverly-Waterloo-Cedar Rapids de-electrified, freight by diesel | (−) March 31, 1957 |
| Waterloo-Cedar Falls | (−) August 1, 1958 |

Line sold to joint Rock Island-Illinois Central, then later, solely Illinois Central and now mostly dismantled. What remains in early 1988 is part of Chicago Central & Pacific.

| | |
|---|---|
| Miles of line | 86 |
| Power system | 1400 v DC trolley and catenary |
| Passenger motor cars at time of photo | 3 |
| Vehicle series shown | 100 - 102 |
| Length over all | 60 ft. 3 in. |
| Weight in tons | 51½ |
| Motors, quantity / builder / rating | 4 / Wh-333E7 / 140 hp |
| Control, single or double end / type | SE / Wh-HL 15E |
| Approximate free speed | 70 mph on 1400 v |
| Builder / year delivered | McGuire-Cummings / 1914 |

This car, built as a parlor-buffet car without control, was one of three shopped in 1927-1928 to become combination baggage-passenger observation coaches. In 1940, when the original 25 hz power system had to be replaced with 60 hz, trolley voltage was raised from 1300 to 1400, pushing up motor horsepower and making extra oomph available to help a late train catch up. However, on the Waterloo-Waverly branch, where this view was taken, 700 v trolley was used and a stately 30-35 mph was normal top speed.

Car 100, the only one with enclosed rear platform, was preserved, first at Centerville, IA and later at Mason City, IA where it was accidentally destroyed by fire November 23, 1967.

DES MOINES & CENTRAL IOWA RAILWAY 1712 ►►

| | |
|---|---|
| Des Moines-Colfax, IA | (+) 1902 |
| Des Moines-Woodward-Perry | (+) 1906 |
| Des Moines-Colfax, Woodward branch | (−) 1941 passenger |
| Des Moines-Colfax, Woodward branch | (−) 1946 freight |
| Granger-Perry | (−) 1948 passenger |
| Des Moines-Granger | (−) 1949 passenger |
| Des Moines-Granger de-electrified | (−) 1949 |
| Granger-Perry | (−) 1954 freight |

| | |
|---|---|
| Miles of line | 61 |
| Power system | 600 v DC trolley |
| Motor cars owned at time of photo | 3 |
| Vehicle series shown | 1710, 1712, 1714 |
| Length over all | 60 ft. 1½ in. |
| Weight in tons | 42½ |
| Motors, quantity / builder / rating | 4 / Wh-557 / 140 hp |
| Control, single or double end / type | SE / Wh ALFM-C36 |
| Approximate free speed | 65 mph (35 by rule) |
| Builder / year delivered | Jewett / 1918 |

After some twenty years of racing along the shore of Lake Erie between Cleveland and Toledo, with side trips to Detroit and to Lima, former Lake Shore Electric Railway cars 170, 179 and 180 were rebuilt with baggage compartments in Iowa in 1939. A sedate (half-speed) career of surprisingly heavy duty throughout World War II followed.

E. VAN DUSEN / July 31, 1948 / Des Moines, IA

### FT. DODGE DES MOINES & SOUTHERN R.R. 362 ▶▶

| | |
|---|---|
| Predecessor segments operated by steam | (+) 1880 -1906 |
| Electric streetcars in Fort Dodge | (+) 1896  (−) 1925 |
| Electrification and extension | |
| Des Moines to Fort Dodge and four branches, in stages | (+) June 1907-1917 |
| Changed from 600 v to 1200 v | (+) September 1911 |
| Passenger services discontinued | |
| Ft. Dodge-Webster City-Lehigh | (−) 1925 |
| Hope-Rockwell City | (−) 1926 |
| Kelly-Ames | (−) 1928 |
| Des Moines-Ft. Dodge, due to flood | (−) June 20, 1954 to November 21, 1954 |
| Des Moines-Ft. Dodge, passenger service | (−) August 31, 1955 |
| System, freight service dieselized | (−) 1949-1955 |

Most of this railroad is now dismantled

| | |
|---|---|
| Miles of line | 147 |
| Power system | 1200 v DC trolley |
| Vehicle series shown | 360 - 362 |
| Length over all | 58 ft. 2 in. |
| Weight in tons | 91 |
| Motors, quantity / type / rating | 8 / GE-205 / 100 hp |
| Control, single or double end / type | DE / GE-M / C90 |
| Approximate free speed | 30 mph |
| Builder / year built | Spokane Portland & Seattle Ry / 1944 |
| Acquired from / year | Oregon Elec. Ry. / 1946 |

This locomotive is shown awaiting call in the small yard at the foot of the gold-domed Iowa State capitol. One of five engines built by an ingenious shop force, 362 utilized motors, control, trucks and other equipment salvaged from interurban passenger cars of the Oregon Electric. But OE dieselization was being programmed even while the work was in progress and thus three of the newly reconstructed products finished their careers as Fort Dodge workhorses while the others did likewise for the North Shore Line.

◄◄ FORT DODGE DES MOINES & SOUTHERN R.R. 62

| | |
|---|---|
| Interurban passenger motor cars, 1940 | 5 |
| Vehicle series shown | 62 |
| Length over all | 55 ft. 6¾ in. |
| Weight in tons | 40 |
| Motors, quantity / builder / rating | 4 / GE-205 / 100 hp |
| Control, single or double end / type | DE / GE-M |
| Approximate free speed | 50 mph |
| Builder / year delivered | American / 1916 |

In view of today's vehicle procurement problems, it may be hard to believe that back before World War I a company could order just one car of a distinctive design for delivery within just a few months. That's exactly what the Fort Dodge line did to buy car 62 and, at the same time, car 52, an entirely different center door type.

This photo was taken during a stopover of a CERA inspection trip on the campus of the state university.

▼ MASON CITY & CLEAR LAKE R.R. 107

| | |
|---|---|
| Mason City-Clear Lake, IA | (+) July 4, 1897 |
| Passenger service discontinued | (−) 1936 |
| Miles of line | 11 |
| Power system | 600 v DC trolley |
| Vehicle series shown | 107 |
| Length over all | 45 ft. 4 in. |
| Weight in tons | 15 |
| Motors, quantity / builder / rating | 4 / GE-80 / 50 hp |
| Control | One K-35 |
| Approximate free speed | 28 mph |
| Builder / year delivered | Tri City Ry shop Davenport, IA / 1923 |

This little railway is a real survivor, having developed a terminal railroad business serving the principal industries in an important rural community. Before the days of good hard roads and private autos it had a reasonably good passenger business between the railroad junction town of Mason City and the recreation area at Clear Lake. At one time it got extra business in winter moving bulk ice sawed from the frozen surface of Clear Lake to ice houses in town.

It went to one-man operation in 1923, using revamped city cars from Davenport, IA. As the Iowa Traction R.R. it continues in 1988 to switch freight, using second-owner Baldwin-Westinghouse engines.

G. KRAMBLES / October 15, 1955 / Mason City, IA

84

**MINNEAPOLIS ANOKA & CUYUNA RANGE R.R. 100**
Northern Pump Company switching line

| | |
|---|---|
| Minneapolis-Anoka MN using McKeen gas cars .. | (+) June 10, 1913 |
| Electrified, extended downtown via Minneapolis St. Ry. .......................... | (+) October 9, 1915 |
| Passenger rail service discontinued ............ | (−) August 23, 1939 |
| Passenger, 30/Marshall-Northern Pump plant .... | (+) Oct. 1943 (−) April 1948 |
| De-electrified / abandoned in steps ............ | (−) August 1957 / et seq |

| | |
|---|---|
| Miles of line .................................. | Approx. 4 |
| Power system ................................. | 600 v DC trolley |
| Locomotives owned, 1953 ...................... | 2 |
| Vehicle series shown .......................... | 100 |
| Length over all ............................... | 36 ft. 10 in. |
| Weight in tons ................................ | 43 |

| | |
|---|---|
| Motors, quantity / builder / rating ............... | 4 / GE205D / 100 hp |
| Control, single or double end / type.............. | DE / GE-M C74F |
| Approximate free speed ....................... | 25 mph |
| Builder / year delivered ........................ | General Electric / 1913 |
| Acquired from / year .......................... | Central Warehouse / 1922 |

This locomotive began as a gas-electric engine of the Minneapolis St. Paul Rochester & Dubuque Electric Traction Company, the Dan Patch Lines, which never operated by trolley, becoming part of the Minneapolis Northfield & Southern RR. Meantime, 100 was sold to the Central Warehouse Company of St. Paul where it was converted for trolley operation. MA&CR bought it in 1922.

During WW II, the Northern Pump Company undertook defense contracting and bought MA&CR, by then a dilapidated shambles. They had Minneapolis Street Railway rehab the equipment they needed, rebuilt 100 becoming new 1, changed back to 100 in 1946. It is preserved at Minnesota Transportation Museum.

T. H. DESNOYERS (G. KRAMBLES) / October 1950 / Minneapolis, MN

◄ MINNEAPOLIS MUNICIPAL WATERWORKS RAILWAY 1
Filtration plant switching line

Soo Line R.R. to filtration plant in
Columbia Hts., (Minneapolis) MN . . . . . . . . . . .  (+) November 1917
Passenger service . . . . . . . . . . . . . . . . . . . . . . . . .  (−) May 1, 1948
All remaining service . . . . . . . . . . . . . . . . . . . . . .  (−) May 15, 1953

Miles of line . . . . . . . . . . . . . . . . . . . . . . . . . . . . . . .  1½
Power system. . . . . . . . . . . . . . . . . . . . . . . . . . . . . . . .  600 v DC trolley
Motor cars, 1953 . . . . . . . . . . . . . . . . . . . . . . . . . . . .  This car, #1, only
Weight in tons . . . . . . . . . . . . . . . . . . . . . . . . . . . . . .  21.5
Motors, quantity / builder / rating . . . . . . . . . . . . . .  4 / GE-73 / 75 hp
Control, single or double end / type. . . . . . . . . . . . . .  DE / GE-M C101A
Approximate free speed . . . . . . . . . . . . . . . . . . . . . .  25 mph
Builder / year delivered . . . . . . . . . . . . . . . . . . . . . .  McGuire-Cummings / 1917

Built before the days of hard roads or private autos, this line brought employees to/from the nearest Twin Cities streetcar line and moved carloads of filtration plant materials such as chlorine and filter sand. When the neighborhood began to build up, the line offered service to the public at 3¢ a ride.

UNIVERSITY OF MINNESOTA 1  ►

St. Paul-Minneapolis, MN Intercampus line . . . . .  (+) November 4, 1914
St. Paul-Minneapolis, MN Intercampus line . . . . .  (−) June 19, 1954

Miles of line . . . . . . . . . . . . . . . . . . . . . . . . . . . . . .  2.5±
Power system . . . . . . . . . . . . . . . . . . . . . . . . . . . . . .  600 v DC trolley
Locomotive cars for freight switching . . . . . . . . . . . .  This car, #1, only
Length over buffer sills . . . . . . . . . . . . . . . . . . . . . . .  37 ft.
Weight in tons . . . . . . . . . . . . . . . . . . . . . . . . . . . . . .  25.5
Motors, quantity / builder / rating . . . . . . . . . . . . . . .  4 / GE-57 / 50 hp
Control . . . . . . . . . . . . . . . . . . . . . . . . . . . . . . . . . . .  GE K-37
Builder/ year built . . . . . . . . . . . . . . . . . . . . . . . . . .  Twin City RT / 1914

This line had been built (at State expense) to provide for passenger access from connecting Twin Cities car lines to and between the Main Campus in Minneapolis and the Agricultural Campus in St. Paul. The University purchased this car for switching cars of coal, fertilizer, livestock and machinery in and out of both campuses.

G. KRAMBLES / May 26, 1953 / St. Paul, MN

G. KRAMBLES / May 26, 1953 / N. Valley City, ND

◄ VALLEY CITY STREET & INTERURBAN RAILWAY Unnumbered locomotive

| | |
|---|---|
| Valley City-N. Valley City, ND | (+) December 18, 1905 |
| Passenger service | (−) 1930s |
| Merged into Soo Line R.R. | (±) June 23, 1953 |
| De-electrified and dieselized | (−) September 23, 1953 |

| | |
|---|---|
| Miles of line | 1.8 |
| Power system | 600 v DC trolley |
| Motor cars, 1953 | This unnumbered car only |
| Length over buffer sills | 37 ft. |
| Motors, quantity / builder / rating | 4 / Wh 306 / 60 hp |
| Control, single or double end / type | DE / GE MK C101A |
| Builder / year built | Twin Cities RT / 1917 |
| Acquired from / year | Mpls An & Cuy Rnge / 1944 |

The tiny Valley City line provided a rail link connecting the town center with the Soo Line and Northern Pacific Railroads, which passed close to, but at greatly different elevations from the town.

This car saw the rails of four electric railways, starting with those of its builder, then of the St. Paul Southern Electric Railway which folded in 1928, next of the Minneapolis Anoka & Cuyuna Range (and Northern Ordnance Co.), and finally, of the Valley City line.

F. E. BUTTS / 1940 / Coffeyville, KS

◄◄ UNION ELECTRIC RAILWAY 84

| Coffeyville-Independence, KA | (+) July 14, 1907 |
| Independence-Cherryvale | (+) March 1, 1910 |
| Cherryvale-Parsons | (+) 1914 |
| Coffeyville, KS-Nowata, OK | (+) 1915 |
| Parsons, KS-Nowata, OK | (−) April 4, 1948 |

| | |
|---|---|
| Miles of line | 77 |
| Power system | 650 v DC trolley |
| Motor passenger / freight / loco, 1940 | 22 / 5 / 5 |
| Vehicle series shown | 84 |
| Length over all | 50 ft. |
| Weight in tons | 50 |
| Motors, quantity / builder / rating | 4 / Wh-562D5 / 100 hp |
| Control, single or double end / type | DE / Wh-HLF-337 |
| Approximate free speed | 25 mph |
| Builder / year delivered | Kuhlman / 1927 |
| Acquired from/ year | C&LERR / 1939 |

With weak traffic potential, Union Electric Railway for years kept down costs by purchasing equipment and supplies second-hand. Box motor 84 (with locomotive propulsion package), which had been built as Cincinnati Hamilton & Dayton (later part of Cincinnati & Lake Erie) 604, was picked up that way.

UE got part of the cost back when it sold 84 to the Sand Springs Railway in Oklahoma, who planned to make it into a line car, but the line crew wanted no part of a steel car so it was never again used.

SAND SPRINGS RAILWAY 73 ▲

| Tulsa-Sand Springs, OK | (+) 1911 |
| Passenger service | (−) January 2, 1955 |
| Dieselized for freight | (−) 1955 |

| | |
|---|---|
| Miles of line | 12 |
| Power system | 600 v DC trolley |
| Passenger cars owned | 10 |
| Vehicle series shown | 71 - 76 |
| Length over all | 45 ft. |
| Weight in tons | 18 |
| Motors, quantity / builder / rating | 4 / Wh-510A / 35 hp |
| Control, single or double end / type | DE / Wh K35kk |
| Approximate free speed | 37 mph |
| Builder / year built | American / 1925 |
| Acquired from / year | Union Electric (of Kansas) 1947 |

This railway started as a means of encouraging suburban development and to help finance a life-long philanthropy of Charles Page, who had struck it rich in the oil and natural gas boom. Page died in 1926 but the railroad kept on supporting the Sand Springs Home for widows and orphans. Carload freight traffic developed to require six Baldwin-Westinghouse B-B steeple cab locomotives, two of them acquired as late as 1947 from the Niagara Junction Railway.

## HUTCHINSON & NORTHERN RAILWAY 1

| | | |
|---|---|---|
| Hutchinson to Carey Mine, KS | . . . . . . . . . . . . . . . . | (+) 1923 |
| De-electrified | . . . . . . . . . . . . . . . . . . . . . . . . . . . . . . . . | (−) February 3, 1970 |
| Miles of line | . . . . . . . . . . . . . . . . . . . . . . . . . . . . . . . . | 6 |
| Power system | . . . . . . . . . . . . . . . . . . . . . . . . . . . . . . . . | 600 v DC trolley |
| Locomotives owned at time of photo | . . . . . . . . . . . . | 3 |
| Vehicle series shown | . . . . . . . . . . . . . . . . . . . . . . . . . . | 1 |
| Length over all | . . . . . . . . . . . . . . . . . . . . . . . . . . . . . . | 28 ft. |
| Weight in tons | . . . . . . . . . . . . . . . . . . . . . . . . . . . . . . | 30 |
| Motors, quantity / builder / rating | . . . . . . . . . . . . . . | 4 / GE-207 / 100 hp |

| | | |
|---|---|---|
| Control, single or double end / type | . . . . . . . . . . . . . . | DE / GE - M |
| Approximate free speed | . . . . . . . . . . . . . . . . . . . . . . . . | 25 mph |
| Builder / year delivered | . . . . . . . . . . . . . . . . . . . . . . . . | General Electric / 1923 |

A family-owned switching railroad connected the family-owned salt mines east of Hutchinson with the Missouri Pacific, Rock Island and Santa Fe railroads. It used about a mile of the Arkansas Valley Interurban Railway (which linked Hutchinson to Wichita). When AVI folded, HN acquired this segment. The locomotive shown had been held in "stock" by GE since 1921.

It is now preserved at the Orange Empire Trolley Museum in Perris, CA.

R. L. DAY / August 22, 1958 / Sapulpa, OK

## TULSA-SAPULPA UNION RAILWAY 202

| | | | |
|---|---|---|---|
| Sapulpa-Mounds, OK | (+) 1908 | (−) 1928 | |
| Sapulpa-Tulsa | (+) 1918, passenger | (−) 1933 | |
| Sapulpa-Tulsa de-electrified | | (−) 1955 | |
| Sapulpa-Tulsa closed | | (−) 1960 | |

| | |
|---|---|
| Miles of line | 25 |
| Power system | 660 v DC trolley |
| Motor cars owned at time of photo | |
| box motors / locomotives | 3 / 3 |
| Vehicle series shown | 202 - 203 |
| Length over all | 50 ft. 4 in. |
| Weight in tons | 43 |

| | |
|---|---|
| Motors, quantity / builder / rating | 4 / Wh-303 / 100 hp |
| Control, single or double end / builder / type | DE / Wh / HL-169 |
| Approximate free speed | 35 mph |
| Builder / year delivered | Cincinnati / 1939 |
| Acquired from / year built | Cincinnati & Lake Erie RR / 1939 |

Despite dreams of a great railroad empire, this little line was never more than a weak suburban line whose life was more than doubled by developing freight switching traffic. This car had been Cincinnati & Lake Erie 648, itself built from the salvage of 1907-vintage passenger interurban cars. When TSU was bought by Borg Compressed Steel Company and dieselized, veteran 202 was acquired by the Seashore Trolley Museum.

G. KRAMBLES / June 7, 1956 / Durant, MT

## BUTTE ANACONDA & PACIFIC RAILWAY 63

| | |
|---|---|
| Butte-Anaconda, MT | (+) 1893 as a steam railway |
| E. Anaconda yard electrified | (+) May 28, 1913 |
| Butte-Anaconda electrified | (+) October 1, 1913 |
| Butte-Anaconda passenger service | (−) April 15, 1953 |
| Entire line, de-electrified | (−) 1967 |
| Miles of line | 32 main line<br>123 all track |
| Power system | 2400 v DC catenary |
| Locomotives owned (1956) | 29 |
| Vehicle series shown | 50 - 66 |
| Length over all | 37 ft. 4 in. |
| Weight in tons | 80 |
| Motors, quantity / builder / rating | 4 / GE-229A / 260 hp |
| Control, single or double end / type | DE / GE-M, C-93 |

| | |
|---|---|
| Approximate free speed | 35 mph freight gearing<br>55 mph passenger gearing<br>discontinued ca. 1947 |
| Builder / year delivered | General Electric / 1913 |

The Butte Anaconda & Pacific was built to move copper ore mined on Butte Hill to the huge smelter at Anaconda and to bring ingots back for distribution to industry. It was a pioneer high-voltage DC electrification, setting the pattern for that of the Chicago Milwaukee St. Paul & Pacific R.R. whose track and 3000 v overhead is along the cliff in the background. Sharing Silver Bow canyon between those two railroads in this scene is the track of the Northern Pacific Railway main line.

In the 1970s foreign competition and technological changes (such as fibre-optics and satellite transmission) started the copper industry into a decline. BAP was acquired by Atlantic Richfield Company, which sold it to the state of Montana in 1984. The uncompetitive CMSP&P line has been dismantled.

H. STANGE / May 27, 1951 / Three Forks, MT

▲ CHICAGO MILWAUKEE ST. PAUL & PACIFIC R.R. E78

| | |
|---|---|
| Butte-Three Forks, MT electrified | (+) December 1, 1915 |
| Harlowton, MT-Avery, ID electrified | (+) 1917 |
| Othello-Tacoma, WA electrified | (+) November 1919 |
| Black River Jct.-Seattle electrified | (+) Summer 1927 |
| Tacoma-Seattle-Othello de-electrified | (−) 1972 |
| Avery-Harlowton de-electrified | (−) June 1974 |
| All above totally abandoned | (−) February 29, 1980 |

| | |
|---|---|
| Miles of line | 660 |
| Power system | 3300 DC catenary |
| Locomotives owned | 128 |
| Vehicle series shown | E70 - E79 |
| Length over all | 87 ft. 9¾ in. |
| Weight in tons | 275 |
| Motors, quantity / builder / rating | 8 / GE-750 / 700 hp |
| Control, single or double end / builder / type | DE / GE / M |
| Approximate free speed | 68 mph |
| Builder / year delivered | General Electric / 1950 |

In 1948-49 GE had under construction 20 high-speed passenger locomotives for Russia's 60-inch gage, 3000 v DC lines. The onset of the "cold war" caused an embargo on delivery and a search for alternative customers. Fifteen were completed in standard gage, three for the Chicago South Shore & South Bend Railroad and twelve for the Milwaukee Road, where ten were geared for freight service and two for passenger. The remaining five units were finished in 63-inch gage and shipped to the Paulista Railway in Brazil.

BAMBERGER RAILROAD 355  ▶▶

| | |
|---|---|
| Salt Lake-Ogden (steam) | (+) August 5, 1908 |
| Line electrified | (+) May 28, 1910 |
| Passenger service discontinued | (−) September 7, 1952 |
| Freight service was changed to diesel; segments abandoned | |

| | |
|---|---|
| Miles of line | 37 |
| Power system | 750 v DC trolley |
| Motor cars at time of photo | 19 |
| Vehicle series shown | 350 - 355 |
| Length over all | 61 ft. 6 in. |
| Weight in tons | 43 |
| Motors, quantity / builder / rating | 4 / GE-205B / 110 hp |
| Control, single or double end / type | DE / GE-PC101A-C36 |
| Approximate free speed | 60 mph |
| Builder / year delivered | Jewett / 1916 |

Originally built as an excursion trailer with unglazed sides, this series was rebuilt at North Salt Lake after a disastrous barn fire on May 7, 1918 destroyed twenty cars and a locomotive as well as the entire Ogden barn. Propulsion and air brake equipment was salvaged from the damaged cars. Steel plates needed to close up the car sides came from a Bamberger-owned mine.

UTAH IDAHO CENTRAL RAILROAD 506  ▶ ▼

| | |
|---|---|
| City lines of Ogden (UT) Rapid Transit | (+) May 19, 1900 |
| Ogden-Hot Springs, UT | (+) 1890s as a steam dummy |
| (Electrified and extended to Brigham) | (+) 1907 |
| Ogden-Plain City | (+) 1909 as a steam line |
| (Electrified) | (+) 1916 |
| (Extended to Warren) | (+) 1918 |
| Canyon line, Ogden to Huntsville | (+) 1909 to 1915 in steps |
| City lines of Logan (UT) Rapid Transit | (+) 1910 |
| Logan-Smithfield | (+) 1910 |
| Providence-Wellsville | (+) 1914-1915 |
| Wellsville-Brigham | (+) 1915 |
| Completed Ogden-Preston, ID and electrification changed 600 to 1500v | (+) October 27, 1915 |
| Sugarton-Quinney (Cache Valley RR) | (+) 1916-1918 |
| Streetcars discontinued in Logan | (−) 1924 |
| Ogden Canyon passenger service | (−) 1932; freight (−) 1935 |
| Ogden local car service | (−) December 26, 1935 |
| Remaining passenger service | (−) Feb. 15; freight (−) Feb. 28, 1947 |

| | |
|---|---|
| Miles of line | ± 110 |
| Power system | 1500 v DC catenary and trolley except 750 v in Ogden |
| Motor cars owned at time of photo, passenger / freight / locomotive | 18 / 3 / 8 |
| Vehicle series shown | 501-517 |
| Length over all | 63 ft. 8 in. |
| Weight in tons | 43 |
| Motors, quantity / builder / rating | 4 / Wh-334E6 / 110 hp |
| Control, single or double end / builder / type | DE / Wh HL - 15E |
| Approximate free speed | 47 mph |
| Builder / year delivered | American / 1915-1918 |

This car design, virtually duplicating Salt Lake & Utah cars built by both American and Niles, shared similar strengths and weaknesses. The UIC fleet seems to have been about triple what was needed.

W. D. MIDDLETON / February 19, 1951 / North Salt Lake, UT

A. R. ALTER (B. BILLINGS) / October 4, 1944 / Ogden, UT

## KENNECOTT COPPER CORPORATION 734

| | |
|---|---|
| Bingham Canyon open pit mine electrified | (+) 1924 |
| de-electrified | (−) September 1983 |
| | |
| Miles of line | ± 150 |
| Power system | 750 v DC side trolley |
| Locomotives owned | 68 |
| Vehicle series shown | 700s |
| Length over all | 38 ft. |
| Weight in tons | 85 |
| Motors, quantity / builder | 4 / GE-818-B |

| | |
|---|---|
| Control, single or double end / builder / type | DE / GE M |
| Approximate free speed | 25 mph |
| Builder / year delivered | General Electric / 1929 |

It was a fantastic operation, reminiscent of an inverted anthill, in the world's largest open-pit copper mine. Locomotives and shovels were powered from the trolley, which was strung along the side of the track away from the hill in areas to be mined using tripod-like line poles that could be shifted along the track as the copper ore was removed. Gradual depletion of the ore compounded by declining market conditions caused rail operations first to be suspended and later to be supplanted by trucking.

## SKAGIT RIVER RAILWAY 89

Rockport to Newhalem, WA .................. (+) 1919-1920
(−) April 4, 1954
Newhalem-Diablo passenger service ............ (+) 1928 (−) 1941
Line dismantled upon completion of hydro-electric project

Miles of line ................................... 31
Power system.................................... 600 v DC trolley
Motor cars owned at time of photo ................ 8
Vehicle shown .................................. 89
Length over all ................................ 44  ft. (estimated)

Weight in tons ................................. 30 (unloaded)
Motors, quantity / rating ....................... 4 / 75 hp

As part of the hydro-electric development for the City of Seattle, a construction railway was built in the gorge of the Skagit River northeast of the city. Part of it was electrified, using second hand rolling stock from abandoned lines in the state.

This motor car is believed to have been built from the salvage of Washington Water Power (Spokane) car 510, acquired in 1922. The railway was closed to the public during World War II and ultimately was torn up when the planned construction was completed.

A. R. ALTER (B. BILLINGS) / May 7, 1945 / Portland, OR

| | | |
|---|---|---|
| Portland-Oregon City, OR | (+) February 16, 1893 | |
| Portland-Gresham-Cazadero | (+) 1903 | |
| Gresham-Troutdale | (+) 1909 | (−) 1931 |
| Montavilla-Bull Run | (+) 1911 | (−) 1927 |
| Gresham-Cazadero | (−) 1933 et seq | |
| Bellrose-Gresham | (−) 1949 | |
| Portland-Oregon City-Bellrose | (−) January 25, 1958 | |

Freight service by diesel continues over certain segments

| | | |
|---|---|---|
| Miles of line, 1945 | Approx. 22 | |
| Power system | 600 v DC trolley | |
| Vehicle series shown | 4000 - 4005 | 4006 - 4007 |
| Length over all | 45 ft. 6 in. | 40 ft. 6 in. |
| Weight in tons | 20 | 21 |
| Motors, quantity / builder / rating | 4 / Wh510E / 35 hp | 4 / GE247I / 40 hp |
| Control, single or double end / type | 2 / WhHL / 15B | 1 / GE / K75 |
| Approximate free speed | 35 mph | 40 mph |
| Builder / year delivered | Kuhlm'n / 1928 | Cinc'i / 1927 |
| Acquired from | PSCo of IN | Fonda J & G |
| Year received in Portland | 1940 | 1942 |

With 65 years of continuous service, the east side interurbans of PEPCO set a remarkable record and now, after nearly thirty years of absence, Portland is enjoying a fine new "light rail" line from downtown to Gresham over a more direct route although using some streets that once had electric cars.

The Indiana cars were bought for New Albany-Jeffersonville-Louisville service and later had worked in Terre Haute. The cars acquired from Fonda Johnstown & Gloversville had been built for the Albany Southern (a 3rd rail line) and had later put in many miles on the Schenectady-Amsterdam-Fonda run. One of the Indiana group is saved at Rio Vista Junction museum.

| | |
|---|---|
| Sacramento-Chico and branches | (+) 1905-1913 in stages |
| Oakland-Sacramento and branches | (+) 1910-1914 in stages |
| Oakland-San Francisco via Bay Bridge | (+) Jan. 15, 1939 |
| Sacramento-Chico and branches | (+) 1905-1913 in stages |
| Oakland-Sacramento and branches | (+) 1910-1914 in stages |
| Oakland-San Francisco via Bay Bridge | (+) Jan. 15, 1939 |
| West Pittsburg-Sacramento-Chico | (−) Passenger, Aug. 26, 1940 |
| San Francisco-Pittsburg | (−) Passenger, July 12, 1941 |

Remainder de-electrified, abandoned bit by bit by 1965

| | |
|---|---|
| Miles of line | 275 |
| Power system | North end 600 v DC third rail except trolley in towns |
| | South end 1500 v DC catenary except 600 v DC trolley on Key tracks and 1200 v DC catenary on Bridge |
| Motor cars owned (1938) passenger / freight / locomotive | 35 / 3 / 21 |
| Vehicle series shown | 650 - 654 |
| Length over all | 35 ft. 6 in. |
| Weight in tons | 61.5 |
| Motors, quantity / builder / rating | 4 / GE-251A / 140 hp |
| Control, single or double end / type | DE / GE - M |
| Approximate free speed | 30 mph |
| Builder / year delivered | General Electric / 1923-1930 |

This view looks north from the gasoline-powered ferry "Ramon," using which the railroad bridged the Suisun Bay tidal basin. A railfan special using MW-302, a former OA&E passenger motor, is in the background. Cautiously, but skillfully, train and boat crews coordinated to cast off ferry and brake train to a stop simultaneously, making up somewhat for "Ramon's" shortage of power. When SN's last electric duty (switching at Marysville-Yuba City) ended in 1965, 654 was donated to the rail museum at Rio Vista Junction.

#### SACRAMENTO NORTHERN RAILWAY MW-302 ► ► ►

| | |
|---|---|
| Vehicle series shown | MW 302, ex 1020 |
| Length over all | 59 ft. |
| Weight in tons | 52 |
| Motors, quantity / builder / rating | 4 / Wh-322E / 140 hp |
| Control, single or double end / builder / type | DE / Wh-HL - 15A2 |
| Approximate free speed | 60 mph |
| Builder / year delivered | Hall Scott / 1913 |
| Year converted from passenger to service | 1941 |

Most of Sacramento Northern had easy grades and curves, but the exception was the ten miles from the east edge of Oakland to Moraga, which included a continuous grade of 2.6% or more and a timber lined tunnel 3200 ft. long. Here a railfan inspection pauses at the substation at the tunnel's east portal. Today this site is lost in suburban housing development. MW-302 was acquired by the Bay Area museum in 1962 to be restored as SN 1020.

G. KRAMBLES / May 31, 1951 / Eastport (Moraga), CA

S. A. GOODRICK (E. VAN DUSEN) / June 1, 1951 / Oakland, CA

KEY SYSTEM 139
Trans-bay (Bridge) lines

Lines to Oakland Key Pier with ferry
service connecting to San Francisco from
    Berkeley Shattuck Ave. (later F line) . . . . . . . . . (+) October 26, 1903
    Piedmont (later C line) . . . . . . . . . . . . . . . . . . . . (+) 1904 ext'd 1924
    22nd St. to Broadway (later B line) . . . . . . . . . . (+) 1906 ext'd 1917
    Claremont (later E line) . . . . . . . . . . . . . . . . . . . (+) April 1, 1908
    12th St. (later A line) . . . . . . . . . . . . . . . . . . . . . (+) 1909, ext'd 1917
    Sacramento St. (later H line) . . . . . . . . . . . . . . (+) June 11, 1911
    Shattuck Ave., Alcatraz-University . . . . . . . . . (−) March 26, 1933
    H line extended to Monterey Ave. . . . . . . . . . . (+) March 26, 1933
Rerouted Oakland-San Francisco via Bay Bridge . (±) January 15, 1939
Train service to Key Pier discontinued . . . . . . . . . (−) October 29, 1939
A line rerouted to Havenscourt . . . . . . . . . . . . . . . (+) March-April 1941
F line extended to Thousand Oaks . . . . . . . . . . . . (+) July-Aug. 1941
Oakland-Richmond via Shipyard Railway . . . . . . (+) Jan. 1943 (−) Sept. 1945
Remaining passenger rail service . . . . . . . . . . . . . . (−) April 20, 1958

Miles of line . . . . . . . . . . . . . . . . . . . . . . . . . . . . . . . Approx. 73

Power system . . . . . . . . . . . . . . . . . . . . . . . . . . . . . . 600 v DC trolley / catenary except overrunning 3rd rail on Bay Bridge
Articulated Bridge units . . . . . . . . . . . . . . . . . . . . . 88
Vehicle series shown . . . . . . . . . . . . . . . . . . . . . . . 136 - 153
Length over all . . . . . . . . . . . . . . . . . . . . . . . . . . . . 110 ft. 5½ in.
Weight in tons . . . . . . . . . . . . . . . . . . . . . . . . . . . . 69
Motors, quantity / builder / rating . . . . . . . . . . . . 4 / GE-66B / 125 hp
Control, single or double end / type . . . . . . . . . . . DE / GE-M C6J
Approximate free speed . . . . . . . . . . . . . . . . . . . . 37 mph
Builder / year delivered . . . . . . . . . . . . . . . . . . . . . Bethlehem + Key shops / 1937

Key's routes while in East Bay communities were like street car lines with little private right-of-way or grade separation. Its crossing of the Bay was free of street traffic or pedestrian interference but had speed-limiting grades. To serve the whole of San Francisco it had only one station. On balance, the Bridge made travel by bus or auto more attractive than using Key trains.

Shown here is the E line terminal between tennis courts in the gardens of the Claremont Hotel which had been built by "Borax" Smith, founder of Key System.

A number of units were acquired by the F.C. General Urquiza and modified by them for service on the Lacroze-Campo de Mayo line in Buenos Aires, Argentina.

**SANTA CRUZ CEMENT CO. 3** ▼
Division of Pacific Cement & Aggregates, Inc.

Davenport-Mine Yard, CA . . . . . . . . . . . . . . . . . . (+) 1924    (−) 1950s

Miles of line . . . . . . . . . . . . . . . . . . . . . . . . . . . . . . ± 3 (36-in gage)
Power system . . . . . . . . . . . . . . . . . . . . . . . . . . . . . . 600 v DC trolley
Motor cars owned, passenger / locomotive . . . . . . . . . . 1 / 2
Vehicle series shown . . . . . . . . . . . . . . . . . . . . . . . . . 3
Motors, quantity / builder / type . . . . . . . . . . . . . . . . 4 / Wh / 906
Approximate free speed . . . . . . . . . . . . . . . . . . . . . . 25 mph
Builder / year delivered . . . . . . . . . . . . . . . . . . . . . . Company shop / 1942

   This railroad was built using mine-type track and equipment acquired second-hand from the Alaska Gatineau Mining Company. This unique passenger car for transporting employees was home-built from salvage of a Cincinnati-built center door interurban combine for the nearby Pacific Coast Railway.

**PACIFIC ELECTRIC RAILWAY 706** ►►
Data below given for Western District
Venice Short Line
Los Angeles-Ocean Park-Venice

Los Angeles-Venice-Ocean Park-Santa Monica . . . (+) In stages 1897-1903
   Track gage changed from 42 in. to 56½ in. . . . . . (+) 1908
   Rail service discontinued . . . . . . . . . . . . . . . . . . . (−) September 17, 1950

Miles of this line . . . . . . . . . . . . . . . . . . . . . . . . . . . . . 17 double track
Power system . . . . . . . . . . . . . . . . . . . . . . . . . . . . . . . . 600 v DC trolley
Vehicle series shown . . . . . . . . . . . . . . . . . . . . . . . . . . 700 - 749
Length over all . . . . . . . . . . . . . . . . . . . . . . . . . . . . . . . 52 ft. 2 in.
Weight in tons . . . . . . . . . . . . . . . . . . . . . . . . . . . . . . . 29
Motors, quantity / builder / rating . . . . . . . . . . . . . . . . 4 / Wh 532AR / 65 hp
Control, single or double end / type . . . . . . . . . . . . . . DE / Wh HL-28E
Approximate free speed . . . . . . . . . . . . . . . . . . . . . . . 40 mph
Builder / year delivered . . . . . . . . . . . . . . . . . . . . . . . Brill / 1925

   Connecting downtown Los Angeles with Santa Monica on the Pacific coast for years offered an attractive target for mass transit, but Pacific Electric was unable to overcome the handicap of slow surface operation over an indirect route. A planned 4th Street subway was to make direct access to the Hill Street tunnel station, but it could not be financed. Today's Southern California Rapid Transit District looks toward building a high speed subway to Santa Monica.

   PE once had 160 cars of the basic design shown, some of which survived to the end of operation of rail service on the Watts line, and a few even ran a few years on Buenos Aires' Campo de Mayo line of the F. C. General Urquiza.

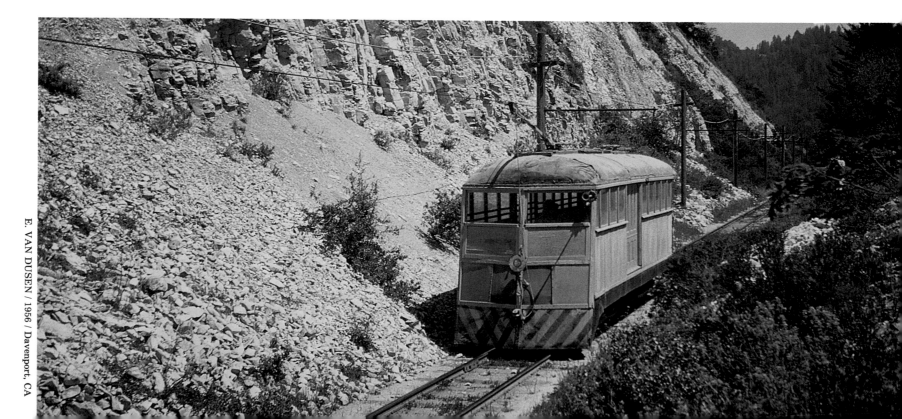

E. VAN DUSEN / 1956 / Davenport, CA

E. VAN DUSEN / May 21, 1949 / Santa Monica, CA

W. D. MIDDLETON / 1951 / Huntington Blvd., El Molino, CA

106

◄ PACIFIC ELECTRIC RAILWAY 1111
Date below given for Northern District
Los Angeles-Monrovia-Glendora line

| | |
|---|---|
| Glendora-Los Angeles | (+) 1902-1907 |
| Passenger service discontinued | (−) September 30, 1951 |
| Certain track retained for diesel freight service | |

| | |
|---|---|
| Miles of line | 26 |
| Power system | 600 v DC trolley |
| Vehicle series shown | 1100 - 1149 |
| Length over all | 42 ft. 4 in. |
| Weight in tons | 48½ |
| Motors, quantity / builder / rating | 4 / GE 240A / 100 hp |
| Control, single or double end / type | DE / GE-PC12D1 |
| Approximate free speed | 47 mph |
| Builder / year delivered | Standard Steel / 1924 |

The last group of interurban cars built for Pacific Electric were the 1100s, acquired to upgrade safety and performance of existing wood-bodied equipment on the Northern District. The unusual double-width vestibules and heavy, high-floored bodies were evidence of parent Southern Pacific's thinking.

Bumped out of service in favor of smaller cars in 1951, the entire lot was sold to Buenos Aires' third-rail powered General Urquiza Railway for additional years of duty. Urquiza also acquired ex-PE 700s and PCCs, not to mention Key System articulated Bridge units, all today replaced by large Japanese-built suburban cars.

▲ PACIFIC ELECTRIC RAILWAY 1374
Date below given for
Northern District, Glendora line only

| | |
|---|---|
| Los Angeles-Pasadena via Oneonta Park | (+) October 1, 1902 |
| Oneonta Park-Monrovia | (+) 1903 |
| Monrovia-Glendora | (+) 1907 |
| Los Angeles-Glendora | (−) September 30, 1951 |

| | |
|---|---|
| Miles of line | 26 |
| Power system | 600 v DC trolley |
| Vehicle series shown | 1372 - 1374 |
| Length over all | 57 ft. |
| Weight in tons | 51 |
| Motors, quantity / builder / rating | 4 / GE-222D / 125 hp |
| Control, single or double end / type | DE / GE PC-101H4-C35H |
| Approximate free speed | 50 mph |
| Builder / year delivered | Pullman / 1913 |

The combination baggage-passenger coach heading this Santa Anita race track special was one of the group acquired in 1928 from the Southern Pacific Railroad's de-electrified Portland (Oregon) interurban network. PE rebuilt them to meet their standards for intercoupling with the 1200-series for working in 600 / 1200 v territory to San Bernardino or on the 600 v Glendora and Pasadena lines.

PACIFIC ELECTRIC RAILWAY 994
Data below given for
Venice Short Line, Western district

| | |
|---|---|
| 4th/Hill, Los Angeles-Vineyard | (+) 1897 |
| Vineyard-Ocean Park | (+) 1902 |
| Venice City Hall-Del Ray | (+) 1903 |
| Track gage changed from 42 in. to 56½ in. | (±) 1908 |
| Name change Los Angeles Pacific to Pacific Electric | (±) 1911 |
| Rail service discontinued | (−) September 17, 1950 |

| | |
|---|---|
| Miles of this line | 17 |
| Power system | 650 v DC catenary or trolley |

| | |
|---|---|
| Motor cars assigned to line (1947) | 35 |
| Vehicle series shown | 950 - 999 |
| Length over all | 49 ft. 2 in. |
| Weight in tons | 37½ |
| Motors, quantity / builder / rating | 4 / GE-73 / 75 hp |
| Control, single or double end / type | DE / GE / M, C-36B |
| Approximate free speed | 48 mph |
| Builder / year delivered | St. Louis / March 31, 1908 |

Originally this car was one of the Los Angeles Pacific series 700-749, built to the distinctive "California" design, that is, about one-third the carbody open, with low screened railings and the remainder in conventional closed fashion with glazed windows. All were rebuilt as fully closed cars and some were "modernized" with divided leather-covered seats and bulls-eye lighting.

PACIFIC ELECTRIC
1005

SAN PEDRO
Via
WEST BASIN

1005

**PACIFIC ELECTRIC RAILWAY 1005**
Date below given for
San Pedro-Los Angeles line, Southern District

| | |
|---|---|
| San Pedro-Wilmington-Los Angeles | (+) 1904-1905-1910 |
| San Pedro-Wilmington-Los Angeles | (−) December 7, 1958 |

| | |
|---|---|
| Miles of line | 25 |
| Power system | 600 v DC trolley |
| Vehicle series shown | 1001 - 1045, 1050 - 1057 |
| Length over all | 55 ft. 6½ in. |
| Weight in tons | 44 |

| | |
|---|---|
| Motors, quantity / builder / rating | 4 / Wh-333A2 / 100 hp |
| Control, single or double end / type | DE / Wh / HL-272-E |
| Approximate free speed | 55 mph |
| Builder / year delivered | Jewett / 1913 |

The 1000s were the first big interurban cars ordered by the Pacific Electric after the so-called "Great Merger", when parent Southern Pacific took over policy direction. They were part of a response to heavy public pressure to relieve overcrowding. They were the first built for 600/1200 v DC service on the then new San Bernardino-Los Angeles line, but they were also the last wooden cars ordered by PE. Car 1001 is preserved at Orange Empire Trolley Museum.

PACIFIC ELECTRIC RAILWAY 450
Data below given for Southern District
Los Angeles-Long Beach line

| | | |
|---|---|---|
| Long Beach-Los Angeles | (+) July 4, 1902 | |
| Passenger service discontinued | (−) April 9, 1961 | |
| Remaining freight trackage dieselized | | |

| | |
|---|---|
| Builder / year delivered | AC&F / 1911 |
| Acquired from / year | U.S. Maritime Comm'n / 1944 |
| Rebuilt and upgraded / year | PE shops / 1948 |

| | |
|---|---|
| Miles of route | 20 |
| Power system | 600 v DC trolley |
| Vehicle series shown | 450 - 459 |
| Length over all | 72 ft. 10 in. |
| Weight in tons | 58 |
| Motors, quantity / builder / rating | 4 / GE-207A / 125 hp |
| Control, single or double end / type | DE / GE-M C-35 |
| Approximate free speed | 40 mph |
| Built for | Southern Pacific R.R.<br>East Bay (Oakland) lines |

These cars were in San Francisco-East Bay service until it was abandoned by Interurban Electric Railway in 1940. Thirty were requisitioned for transporting wartime shipbuilding workers between Los Angeles and Terminal Island yards and later Pacific Electric bought them. The 1948 rebuilding dressed them up substantially, changing the barren 3-2 rattan seating to comfortable 2-2 upholstered, wider spaced seats. Nevertheless, they were sluggish in performance although high in capacity and survived to the end of Long Beach service in 1961, by then operated under the name Los Angeles Metropolitan Transit Authority. During these various stages car numbers were changed several times.

As we go to press, track is being laid by the Los Angeles County Transit Commission for a renaissance light rail line over much the same route.

E. VAN DUSEN / November 6, 1947 / Lyon at McCarty St., Houston, TX

MISSOURI PACIFIC LINES (Houston North Shore Ry.) 524
Electric Div. Beaumont Sour Lake & Western Ry.

| | |
|---|---|
| Houston-Goose Creek, TX | (+) July 19, 1927 |
| Houston-Goose Creek, TX de-electrified | (−) September 25, 1948 |
| Miles of line | 33½ |
| Power system | 600 v DC trolley and catenary |
| Motor cars owned at time of photo | 5 |
| Vehicle series shown | 523 - 526 |
| Length over all | 45 ft. 6 in. |

| | |
|---|---|
| Weight in tons | 19 |
| Motors, quantity / builder / rating | 4 / GE-265 / 35 hp |
| Control, single or double end / type | SE / GE-K75A |
| Approximate free speed | 40 mph |
| Builder / year delivered | American / 1927 |

One of the last interurban railways ever built, this line became a vital oil traffic freight generator for parent Missouri Pacific. When de-electrified, it continued a token passenger service using Twin Coach buses equipped with Evans Auto-Railer devices to permit them to run like today's high-rail vehicles on track or street.

J. W. HIGGINS / November 10, 1952 / Torreon, Coahuila, Mexico

## FERROCARRIL ELECTRICO DE LERDO A TORREON 12

| | |
|---|---|
| Lerdo (Durango)-Torreon (Coahuila), Mexico | (+) 1890 |
| Lerdo (Durango)-Torreon electrified | (+) 1899 |
| Lerdo (Durango)-Torreon | (−) |

| | |
|---|---|
| Miles of line | 15 |
| Power system | 550 v DC catenary |
| Passenger / freight motor cars, 1927 | 19 / 5 |
| Vehicle series shown | 12 |
| Length over all | approx. 32 ft. |

| | |
|---|---|
| Weight in tons | approx. 14 |
| Builder / year | Company shop / 1946 |

Certainly an anomaly to have been built so recently, or for that matter, to have been operating then, the car is believed to have been built from former San Antonio, TX cars. As recently as 1948 the Torreon line reported having an amazing total of 30 motored and 16 non-motored 4-wheeled cars, plus two powered "cab-on-a-raft" flat cars to bump along over its 56-lb. rails. It's gone now.

W. C. JANSSEN / January 8, 1959 / Esperanza, Puebla, Mexico

**FERROCARRIL MEXICANO 1012**
Merged into Nacionales de Mexico from 1960

Electrified
Esperanza-Orizaba . . . . . . . . . . . . . . . . . . . . . . . . . . (+) October 6, 1924
Orizaba-Cordoba . . . . . . . . . . . . . . . . . . . . . . . . . . . . (+) 1926
Cordoba-Paso del Macho . . . . . . . . . . . . . . . . . . . . . . . (+) May, 1928
De-electrified Experanza-Paso del Macho . . . . . . . . (−) 1974

Miles of line . . . . . . . . . . . . . . . . . . . . . . . . . . . . . . . . . 70 (112 km)
Power system . . . . . . . . . . . . . . . . . . . . . . . . . . . . . . . . 3000 v DC catenary
Locomotives owned . . . . . . . . . . . . . . . . . . . . . . . . . . . 12
Vehicle series shown . . . . . . . . . . . . . . . . . . . . . . . . . . 1001 - 1012
Length over all . . . . . . . . . . . . . . . . . . . . . . . . . . . . . . . 52 ft. 11 in.

Weight in tons . . . . . . . . . . . . . . . . . . . . . . . . . . . . . . . . 154.5
Motors, quantity / builder / rating . . . . . . . . . . . . . . . 4 / GE-278A / 460 hp
Control, single or double end / type . . . . . . . . . . . . . . DE / GE / regenerative
Approximate free speed . . . . . . . . . . . . . . . . . . . . . . . 19.5 mph (32 kph)
Builder / years delivered . . . . . . . . . . . . . . . . . . . . . . GE / 1924-1929

About to descend the thirty miles of severe grade from the high central plateau of Mexico to the coastal plains on a route extending from Mexico City to Vera Cruz, a pair of B°-B°-B° locomotives provided the regenerative power needed to control this eastbound train on the 4.7% ruling (5.25% uncompensated) slope. To make today's diesel operation practical, a major line relocation has been planned.

F. J. GOLDSMITH, Jr. / October 1954 / Hershey Central, Cuba

## FERROCARRIL CUBANO DE HERSHEY 107

| | |
|---|---|
| Casa Blanca (Havana)-Matanzas and branches . . . | (+) 1920-1921 |
| Casa Blanca-Cojimar . . . . . . . . . . . . . . . . . . | (−) 1957 |
| Santa Cruz del Norte-Jibacoa . . . . . . . . . . . . | (−) 1960s |

| | |
|---|---|
| Miles of line . . . . . . . . . . . . . . . . . . . . . . . . | 80 |
| Power system . . . . . . . . . . . . . . . . . . . . . . . . | 1200 v DC catenary |
| Motor cars 1954, passenger / freight / locomotive . . . . . | 17 / 4 / 11 |
| Vehicle series shown . . . . . . . . . . . . . . . . . . | 100 - 109 |
| Length over all . . . . . . . . . . . . . . . . . . . . . . . | 49 ft. 3 in. |
| Weight in tons . . . . . . . . . . . . . . . . . . . . . . . | 29 |

| | |
|---|---|
| Motors, quantity / builder / rating . . . . . . . . . . . . . . . | 4 / GE-263 / 65 hp |
| Control, single or double end / builder / type . . . . . . . . | DE / GE / PC |
| Approximate free speed . . . . . . . . . . . . . . . . . . . . . . | 39 mph |
| Builder / year delivered . . . . . . . . . . . . . . . . . . . . . | Brill / 1919 |

Built to serve the sugar plantations and refinery of the famous chocolate company, Hershey Cuban has brought many a railfan to Cuba over the years. Today it remains an active segment of the now-nationalized Ferrocarriles Cuba. Much of the original car and electrical equipment continues in daily service. For example, 107 shown here is 3107 today as it nears its 70th birthday.

# THE SINGLE TRUCK

Development of single-truck cars led to increasingly longer car bodies in turn requiring the use of suitable long wheelbase trucks. Review of thirty-five post-1930 European cars, i.e. cars built years after this vehicle type ceased to be of interest to U.S. operators, shows that with the overall body length varying between 28'-8" and 36'-4" and that of the truck wheelbase between 7'-4" and 10'-6" the ratio of body length to wheelbase ranged between 3.3 and almost 4. In other words the body was some 3 to 4 times as long as the wheelbase. This calls for particular attention to be paid to the truck design to insure good riding qualities at speeds of up to about 25 mph, the aim being low natural frequencies and reduced amplitudes of pitching. This in turn calls for reasonably soft and well (but not too well) damped suspensions. Good riding qualities in the lateral plane on tangent track require well-controlled wheelsets, both laterally as well as fore-and-aft, while curve negotiation benefits from a certain degree of freedom which perforce is limited by the axle-hung motor.

The art of producing an all-round satisfactory truck consists in reconciling these contradictory but interdependent requirements to ensure a simple, reliable, effective, and undemanding design. According to Prof. Walter Reichel, inventor of the bow current collector and designer of numerous street cars and highly successful electric locomotives, a good design produces a truck that could be repaired with a hammer. The chairman of the Australian State Railways once said that even that was too demanding; a well placed kick should suffice!

Considering the available suspension springs it is important to assess the weights of the working part of each type, even if small compared with that of the complete vehicle. Of course, comparing the active weight does not take into account that of the inactive masses such as the buckle of leaf springs, the dead end windings of the coil springs, the clamped ends of torsion bars or the spring securing and carrying components. In other words, here a comparison is made of the weight of the spring proper only. Taking the weight of the torsion bar spring, as recently used with a number of Swiss street and interurban cars as 1.0, that of the helical spring works out as 1.8, that of the coned disc or Belleville spring as 6, the volute spring (for example as used with the early Westend trucks) as 10 and that of the leaf spring as 15. In Flexicoil form, helical springs acting in the horizontal plane replace the swing links and bolster beams, while a leaf spring acting as a supporting beam reduces the bending stresses otherwise imposed on frame members.

In the early days the helical spring was quite helpless in damping oscillations excited by the track. Its time came with the development of reliable hydraulic dampers, but in the meantime use had to be made of whatever was available and this happened to be the leaf spring which could be used as a spring, a damper, or both. Leaf spring performance is dependent upon the magnitude of friction forces adversely affecting its performance as a spring and benefitting it by damping due to interleaf friction $f$, the number of leaves $n$, their thickness $h$, total length $2L$ and the load at one end $P$. It was E. E. Noltein, the chief mechanical engineer of the Moscow-Kasan Railway, who in 1892 derived the lead spring friction force as

$$P_f = f(n-1)Ph/L$$

but this was published in Russia only so that it was left to A. Marie to publish the widely known French derivation of 1905. The crux is $f$ which with four-wheel wagon springs ranges from about 0.12 when new to about 0.3 after four years in service.

With hydraulic damping a dimensionless damping factor of about 0.25 insures oscillation decay within about 3 cycles, this being desirable in terms of passenger comfort as well as the time between succeeding excitations. With friction damping the corresponding value should not exceed 0.9 obtained dividing maximum friction force by the spring constant and by the amplitude of the exciting oscillation emanating from the track. It may be impossible to get an all round satisfactory, friction damping under all operating conditions, particularly since a damping factor of 0.75 would substantially reduce the damper effectiveness. Since the friction force will depend on $f$ and on the excitation force coming from the track, it stands to reason that careful adjustment and maintenance are called for and that all that can be expected is a certain known improvement of the riding qualities.

Similar considerations apply to the friction damping expected of the link suspension as used with pre-World War I street cars in Austria and Hungary. The scatter likely to be encountered in service is indicated by wagon tests carried out by the writer:

| Example | Lateral interleaf friction at full load | |
|---|---|---|
| | New | Worn |
| A | 0.092 - 0.088 | 0.082 - 0.076 |
| B | 0.055 - 0.041 | 0.110 - 0.080 |

However, this information was not available until some fifteen years after World War II and in the meantime, reliable hydraulic dampers permitted the application of helical and air springs to double truck and articulated cars. There was a corresponding loss of interest in the four-wheelers. The most successful single truck, the 21-E dating back to 1895, was evolved by John A. Brill. In 1899 Brill drew attention to the eight springs above the frame fitted "on each side of the journal boxes, and half-elliptic springs on the ends of the extension pieces. These springs have the peculiar characteristic of overcoming any regular motion that may be set up. They utterly refuse to vibrate, and, having once yielded to a blow, return at once to their normal condition without a repetition of flexure".

Similar views were expressed by Brill's President, James Rawle (1842-1912), when he explained that "A serious difficulty, which for a long time baffled all attempts to overcome, was the bouncing motion, or oscillation, of the car body. There was evidently something wrong with the spring system. We were the first to recognize that the difficulty lay in the fact that the rail joints produced a rhythmic motion in the coil springs; we, therefore, introduced slower acting elliptical springs. It was necessary to lengthen the extensions and mount the elliptical springs on the extensions, thus breaking the rhythm set up by the coil springs, and to a large extent preventing oscillations. At the same time, the elliptical springs extended the spring base. Later on the full-elliptical springs were superseded by semi-elliptics, which still farther extended the spring base and were slower acting".

Another twenty years had to pass before the vibrational aspects of vehicle design became common knowledge, but in the meantime, it would have been possible to ascertain the natural frequencies and damping properties of vehicle suspensions with the aid of very simple, if not primitive equipment and the simple expedient of a single excitation impact generated by running the car concerned over wedges under all wheels. However, in spite of rather simplistic interpretation of vehicle vibrations Albert G. Brill succeeded in producing the beautifully simple, reliable and technically "right" 21-E truck. It remained the "world's standard" throughout the time of four-wheel cars from 1895 onwards. It met the standard cited in 1877 by A. M. Wellington (1847-1895) in his book *The Economic Theory of the Location of Railways* that, "It would be well if engineering were less generally thought of, and even defined, as the art of constructing. In a certain important sense it is rather the art of not construction; or to define it rudely but not inaptly, it is the art of doing that well with one dollar, which any bungler can do with two after a fashion". Here the Brill truck was a one dollar solution!

Similar trucks were produced for world wide use by the Peckham Company of Kingston, New York. Most European makers turned to fabricated or pressed steel frames using leaf springs fitted under or over the axleboxes and between truck and the car body, the wheelbase generally ranging between 78" and 99" with 29'-33' long bodies. A move away from the separate truck came in 1924 when the Berlin Street Railway, having increased curve radius to at least 100 ft acquired 500 motor and 800 trailer cars with running gear consisting of axle guides extending from the underframe, the body being carried by leaf springs, with auxiliary end coil springs, mounted on the axle boxes. The 32'-10" long and 86½" wide, 11t cars had a wheelbase of 110¼", increased to 126" with subsequent orders, power being provided by two 45 hp motors. The identical trailers weighed 7½ tons and accommodated 24 seated and 46 standing passengers, some six more than the motorcar. With these cars, designed by the company's chief rolling stock engineer, E. Kindler, the deflection of the suspension, due to heavy load at end stops, could and did cause the brakes to release due to the brake blocks being lowered clear of the wheels. To prevent this the hand brake of the motor cars was applied via internally expanding pads applied to automotive type drums on the motor shaft while the trailers were fitted with two discs on each axle with a pad-applying toggle gear between these, later to be superseded by the first ever disc brakes solenoid activated in normal service.

Vienna Street Railways, which up to the end of World War I did not favor separate trucks, also used axle guides extending from the underframe. The body was carried by leaf springs and long inclined links permitting lateral and limited longitudinal wheelset displacement to facilitate curve negotiation of the 144″ wheelbase 11-12t cars. To meet the occasional demand for longer wheelbase, Brill offered about 1912 the "Radiax" truck while in 1910 the St. Louis Car Co. took up the similar Warner version, referred to as the non-parallel axle truck. Both designs relied on the nose of the axle-hung motor to act as the pivot about which the wheelset would turn in curves. The axlebox carried the truck frame via coil springs and short side hangers. Steering was effected by flange forces and centrifugal force exerted by the car body. Like all such designs, these were not very effective. The forces in curves depended on street traffic density and drivers skill. They had a tendency to nose uncontrollably on tangent track. Neither design was particularly popular and the number of cars thus equipped remained relatively small.

In Europe the design of self-steering single axle trucks, possibly promoted by the 1889 appearance of Robinson's six-wheeler, for a while became a national pastime of German, Swiss and Belgian builders and operators. M.A.N.'s single-axle trucks became the most widely used ones with a total of 422 cars (some 220 for Russia) thus equipped between 1901 and 1914. The six-wheel design of Jacob Buchli, the ingenious general manager of the Swiss Locomotive Works, was used in small numbers with a few Swiss undertakings and with some twelve German street railways. Munich acquired them for some 290 motor cars and 225 trailers. These were all 43′-6″ long with 20′-4″ wheelbase. The motor cars were powered by 100-140 hp motors, two per car and weighed 16.3-17.4 tons. The trailers weighed 11-12 tons.

Compared with conventional single or double truck cars the Buchli and similar trucks did not meet expectations since the steering of the end axles by the middle one, while of benefit in curves, did occur fully only with the car completely in the curve. Not many curves were much longer than the trucks. Furthermore, the middle wheelset with its 20″-24″ wheels tended to hunt rather violently at speed, setting up intense car oscillations. Attempts made to eliminate this led to the use of cylindrical treads on the middle wheels, but these tended to run up against one of the rails, this being also the case when individually mounted wheels were tried. It seems probable that in the future design work will be concentrated on the four-wheel running gear for single, double-truck or articulated cars.

J. L. K.

## TRACTIVE RESISTANCE

Tractive resistance considerations relating to the design of interurban cars became, after relatively tranquil years devoted to rational development along utilitarian lines, bedevilled by the fad for streamlining or streamstyling. With interurbans, paint schemes suddenly became a great exuberant answer to the demand for modernization. Some cars sedately moving along congested city or suburban streets were made with paint to resemble ships in stormy seas. Most of this seems now to belong to the past.

The air resistance of a chosen car shape is expressed by the relevant drag coefficient $C_d$, which in turn is determined by the drag force $D$ in $lb$ opposing the motion, the vehicle speed $V$ in $ft$ per $sec$, the frontal area of the vehicle $A$ in $ft^2$ and the air density $d$ in $lb\ sec^2/ft^4$. For air

$$d = 0.00238\ lb\ sec^2/ft^4.$$

Since tractive resistance considerations preferably relate to speeds in $mph$, the air resistance component can be expressed in $lb.$ as

$$D = C_d \times 0.26A \times (V/10)^2$$

where $A$ is the frontal area in $sq\ ft$ and $V$ the speed in $mph$.

It will be noted that to keep the air resistance low, it will be desirable to keep $A$ and $C_d$ small. For representative modern streetcars, the projected frontal area is generally in the order of

$$A = 85\ sq\ ft$$

as compared with about

$$A = 100\ sq\ ft$$

for interurbans. The value of the drag coefficient depends on the car end shapes, as well as the various discontinuities represented by ventilators, roof, and underfloor mounted equipment, steps, current collector gear, and so on. Generally, for modern cars

$$C_d = 0.6$$

so that for street cars air resistance

$$D = 0.1325V^2,$$

while for interurbans

$$D = 0.156V^2$$

Rolling resistance, practically identical for street and interurban cars, will claim about 5.5 lb per ton so that the tractive resistance faced by a modern 20 ton streetcar running at 30 mph in the face of a 10 mph wind will add up to

$$R = 5.5 \times 20 + 0.1325\ (30 + 10)^2 = 322\ lb.$$

The required motor power will depend on motor-to-wheels efficiency $e$.

Assuming sensible individual axle drives, $e = 0.95$ so that required power is derived as

$$N = (R \times V)/(375 \times e)$$

where $N$ is $hp$, $R$ is $lb$ and $V$ is mph. For the example streetcar, then

$$N = (322 \times 30)/(375 \times 0.95) = 27\ hp$$

This increases to about 50 hp at 40 mph. Going up a 5% grade will require an additional 100 lb per ton which for the car concerned means a further

$$N = 2000 \times (30 + 10)/(375 \times 0.95) = 225\ hp$$

bringing at 30 mph the total to 252 hp.

This, together with the power required for acceleration explains power demands of modern streetcars and the difficulties faced by some undertakings whose substations are not quite up to it.

In the case of the modern 25 ton interurban car carrying a 3 ton load at 75 mph, the tractive resistance, again in the face of a 10 mph wind, will amount to

$$R = 5.5 \times 28 + 0.6 \times 0.26 \times 100\ (85/10)^2 = 1280\ lb.$$

which will demand

$$N = (1280 \times 75)/(375 \times 0.95) = 270\ hp$$

at the motors. Negotiating a 1% upward grade would increase the resistance by 615 lb which, in turn, would raise the output demand to a total of 400 hp. This corresponds to the weight-frontal area-drag coefficient and the available power output of the "Red Devil" cars of the Cincinnati and Lake Erie Railroad.

In the case of automobiles, the rolling resistance even on good roads is some six to seven times higher than that of rail vehicles. The drag coefficient of motor cars amounting to about $0.8$ in the 1920s had dropped to about $0.55$ by the start of World War II and is now about $0.45$ with most modern cars, some managing to come as low as $0.3$. With buses, the values range between $0.5$ and $0.8$ and with trucks between $0.65$ and $0.9$.

J. L. K.

# TREAD AND FLANGE CONTOUR — A NEGLECTED DETAIL?

The intensive development of electric railway equipment has resulted in a marked improvement of the reliability of most components, both mechanical and electrical, to the stage that the mileage between vehicle overhauls is mainly determined by wheel wear. Because of this greater efforts are called for to reduce tire wear and to cut down the required rectification to a minimum by adopting a tire profile resembling the worn shape. Thus the vibration excitation pattern will remain substantially identical throughout, and the periods between wheel profile attention will be markedly extended. A further benefit will be secured by retaining the "cold rolled" tread and flange contours. With most modern vehicles brake blocks have been replaced by dynamic braking with disc brakes used for holding at stops, so that tread and flange contours should, if suitably designed, last markedly longer than ever before.

The problems involved were rather forcefully brought to the writer's attention by the early trials of British Railways (B R) Freightliner trains introduced to serve container traffic at 75 mph. Use was made of a reputedly well-proven and widely used truck design derived from the cast steel Diamond version. It consists of side frames resting directly on axleboxes and connected by a well-fitting bolster resting on nests of coil springs with somewhat crude friction dampers. These trucks were acquired in appreciable numbers and were assembled under bare platforms. Tests showed that the riding qualities in the horizontal plane were unacceptable at anything above about 60 mph. At 75 mph the ride was dangerously violent with the wheel flanges regularly striking the rails with a bang, a pattern referred to by some European railroads as zig-zag riding, with the accent on the *g* just to emphasize the point. The proposed date of service starting was about to be abandoned. The truck suppliers, summoned in haste, could only stand there in sorrow to say that "we have never witnessed anything like it!"

At this point I thought of the work due to Prof. Dr. Ing. Dr. Ing. h.c. Hermann Heumann (1878-1967), one time works manager of the Prussian State Railways, from 1920 to 1944 Professor of Railway Mechanical Engineering at the Technical University at Aachen and 1948 to 1953 at Munich. His fundamental and far reaching contributions clarified the determination of the direction and magnitude of the forces faced by railroad vehicles on their passage through curves and it was his detailed analysis of rational flange and tread contour design which commanded attention as far as the Freightliner riding was concerned. His particular contribution in this field had a somewhat peculiar origin. Back in 1928 the Netherlands Railways asked the Central European Railway Association (another CERA!) to reconsider the prevailing tire contours. A committee was formed of specialists secured from the German, Austrian, Hungarian and Netherland State Railways. Their findings and recommendations claimed fifteen pages of the April 1, 1934, issue of the prestigious German "Organ for the Advancement of Railway Matters". In this, on the basis of extensive mathematically underpinned considerations, it was proposed to change to a flange contour incorporating an angle of 54°-55° and 1:20-1:10 tread.

These proposals seemed rather absurd to Prof. Heumann. He looked into this matter further and in the September 15, 1934 issue of the "Organ" there appeared his findings (extending over six pages) to demolish, once and for all, the committee's arguments and proposals which disappeared without a trace. Heumann's approach was based on the demand for maximum safety against a derailment, good riding qualities and reduced sliding forces between wheels and rails to reduce wear, at the same time aiming at contour rectification, i.e. tire turning resulting in minimal material losses. He pointed out that instead of *reducing* the prevailing 60° flange angle to 54°, it should be *increased* to 70° to augment the resistance against rail climbing. Thus, at representative friction value of 0.35 at the flange, the ratio of the lateral flange force $Y$ to the wheel load $Q$ would, at 70° flange angle, will be

$$Y/Q = 1.2$$

compared with 0.85 at 60°. If for some reason, such as uneven track, friction affected springs, uneven load distribution, running out of a superelevated curve, or a combination of these factors, the leading, (usually the inner) wheel is unloaded by the track

"falling away from under it", the wheel load loss can, with typical modern trucks, be as high as 55% with 70° flange angle but only about 30% with one of 60°.

Heumann also pointed out that safety against derailment will be improved by inserting a straight section between the fillet joining the contour of the flange to the tread and the flange tip thus increasing the length of the path which the wheel must climb to the top of the rail, as compared with that of the then prevailing flange contours made up of two radii.

As for the riding qualities Heumann stressed that it was somewhat naive to use coned treads in conjunction with convex railheads since wear will hollow out one and flatten the other. It would be better to match both to reduce wear and insure one point contact in place of the prevailing two-point pattern. With the latter the wheel rolls on a point moving laterally across the railhead until the flange contacts the rail at a lower

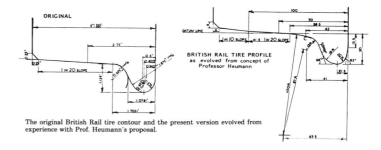

When forced against the rail, the flange contour developed by Prof. Heumann maintains one point of contact throughout thus insuring better riding qualities and reduced wear. The straight section between tread-to-flange fillet and flange tip increases resistance to rail climbing.

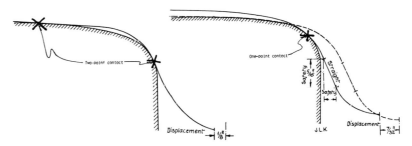

The original British Rail tire contour and the present version evolved from experience with Prof. Heumann's proposal.

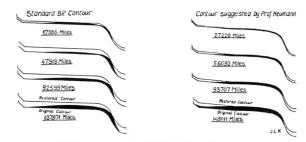

The wear pattern of 48" diameter wheels of the British Rail 80 ton, 100 mph *BoBo* electric locomotives shows the advantages of Prof. Heumann's tire contour. The wear pattern limits future wheel truing mostly to outer tread and flange tip areas.

point, mostly with an impact followed by a scraping wear at the resultant larger radius. The resultant wear pattern is very different from the original contour resulting in subsequently rather wasteful rectification. To counteract this Heumann suggested that the tire contour should insure even wear over the rolling surface and a one-point contact throughout lifting the wheel if need be, by up to about ¼″ if forced by a lateral force moving the point of contact into the flange fillet, this insuring even wear and a shockless contact between flange and rail. While these observations were eminently logical and attractive they hurt CERA's self respect with the result that Heumann was ostracized until 1942 when he received high awards for work published in 1936-1937. In 1943 the German and subsequently the Swiss railways adopted tire contours suggested by him for their locomotives.

These, in general terms, were the ideas which in March 1963 made me ask Prof. Heumann for proposals for a suitable Freightliner tire contour. Within a month detailed drawings were to hand but any reimbursement was declined since "it was fun, I am glad to have been of some use and this is quite sufficient". Applied to a Freightliner wagon the new contour provided the cure much to the relief of all concerned while the then British Rail chairman Dr. Richard (later Lord) Beaching remarked "why has this not been introduced forty years ago?" Encouraged by these results and impressed by Prof. Heumann's logic, I had the new contour used with some, then still running, B R Pullman cars, diesel electric trains and 5100 hp, 100 mph, 80 ton, Bo-Bo electric locomotives with axlehung motors and 48″ diameter wheels. The results speak for themselves not only in terms of reduced wear but also by permitting the retention of the "cold rolled" surfaces, of appreciable value in extending the mileage between overhauls.

Considerations relating to the track work resulted in some changes of the original proposal but the action taken at the time led to the promulgation of the now standard B R tire contour derived from Prof. Heumann's original proposal. Thus, designers and users of street and interurban rolling stock might use a "worn" tire contour along the above lines to improve safety and riding qualities and to reduce wear. This is particularly applicable to designs such as the most recent Geneva, Switzerland, articulated cars with 14¾″ diameter wheels under the middle truck.

J. L. K.

## WHEEL FORCES IN CURVES

While the Vogel method of considering the location of vehicles in curves offered an accurate and convenient way of checking overhang and truck rotation relative to the car body, it was the Minimum Force Method evolved by Prof. Dr. Ing. Dr. Ing. h.c. Hermann Heumann (1878-1967) which insured a simple and reliable determination of the flange forces and of the wear encountered in curves. These considerations were first dealt with in a paper published in 1913. The work continued in ever greater detail and depth, Heumann's last contribution to this subject relating to a paper presented by the writer to the Institution of Locomotive Engineers in 1963. It was essentially due to Heumann that the forces acting between wheels and rails became the subject of rigorous scientific research and that, particularly in recent years, the design of tire profiles has been subjected to detailed examination leading to shapes insuring a marked increase in safety at the same time resulting in a substantial reduction of wear.

Without considering the involved reasoning leading to the investigative methods developed by Heumann, this description is limited to the procedure as related to a typical 6 ft wheelbase standard gauge truck. To quote Oliver Heaviside, "Shall I refuse my dinner because I do not fully understand the process of digestion?"

To begin with it is important to determine the magnitude of the rail directing force $P$ which is the force acting upon the wheel flange at the point of its contact with the rail. In the case of the truck "free wheeling" through the curve, $P$ will act at the outer leading wheel running at a constant speed while the flanges of both rear wheels are

running freely within the channel resulting from the combined clearance width $c$ between both flanges and railheads. To determine the magnitude of $P$ it is necessary to know the wheelload $Q$ and the coefficient of transverse sliding friction encountered by the tread on its passage through the curve as well as the location of the friction force center $M$ of the truck which is the axis about which the four wheels slide on their run through the curve. To locate this it is necessary to plot the Heumann minimum force curve. The truck is drawn in plan view as a "skeleton" to a suitable scale usually 1 in 24. A number of arbitrary points $a_1$, $a_2$, along with the longitudinal axis $x$-$x$ are connected with the wheel tread points on the rails which, for standard gauge, are 4′11″ apart. Following this plot $q_1 + q_2$ vertically upwards from $a_1$, $q_3 + q_4$ from $a_2$ and so on, the resultant points connected provide Heumann's minimum force $M$-curve.

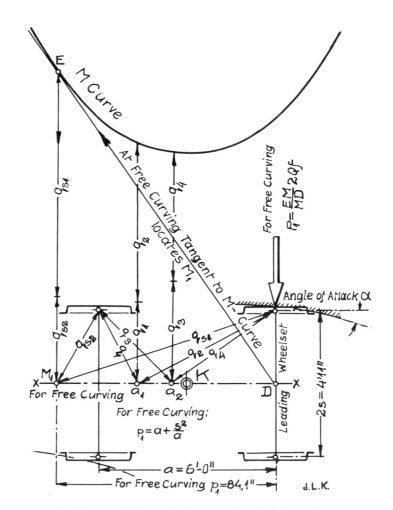

The $M$ curve plotted for any wheel arrangement is used to determine flange forces in curves and resultant flange and tread wear. The initial location of $M$ near the rear axle accounts for the substantially reduced $(DK/p_1)$ impact action at the kingpin $K$ faced at curve entry.

The location of the friction force center about which the truck turns on its way through the curve is also the point common to all friction forces between the truck wheels and the rails. The location of $M$ of the truck free wheeling through the curve is obtained by plotting the tangent from the leading wheelset center at $D$ to the $M$-line, thus locating $E$,$A$ vertical from this down onto the truck longitudinal axis $x$-$x$ provides $M_1$, the distance

$$p_1 = M_1D = a + s^2/a$$

which is the directing arm of the directing force $P$ as well as the wheel slide arms $q_{s_1}$ and $q_{s_2}$. The size of the rail directing force imposed on the leading outer wheel is obtained as

$$P_1 = (EM_1/M_1D)2Qf_s.$$

This must deal with the axle load $2Q$ and must overcome the resistance due to the lateral slip friction having a coefficient of $f_s$. The magnitude of the latter depends on the wheel load and the angle of attack $\alpha$ at which the wheel runs against the rail. Extensive road and rail tests have shown that $f_s$ can be as high as 0.5 but for the loads considered here, 0.45 can be accepted as a representative value. The angle at which the flange of the leading wheel runs up against the rail is obtained as

$$\alpha_1 = p_1/R$$

where $\alpha$ is referred to as the angle of attack and $p_1$ is the directing arm of the force $P_1$ while $R$ is the curve radius. For constrained curving the angle of attack of the inner trailing wheel is derived as

$$\alpha_2 = p_2/R = (a - p_1)/R$$

with

$$p_2 = DM_2 = a - p_1$$

where $M_2$ is the relevant friction force center.

$$\text{Flange wear } W = P\alpha f_f k/r$$

where $f_f$ is the coefficient of flange to rail friction, generally taken as 0.25, while $k$ is a factor relating to the magnitude of the flange angle. Thus for a flange angle of $60°$, $k = 2.3$ as compared with 3.2 for an angle of $70°$, while $r$ is the wheel radius. Thus wear considerations would call for a flange angle of $60°$, although the wear pattern and safety considerations relating to resistance against derailment give preference to the $70°$ flange angle. The equation for $W$ indicates why so much effort has been devoted throughout the years to reduce $\alpha$ with steered wheelsets and also to development of reliable flange lubricators to reduce $f_f$.

In constrained curving the flange of the outer leading wheel runs against the outer rail and the trailing inner wheel runs against the inner rail. Whether constrained curving applies is determined by the magnitude of the directing arm $P_1$ of the leading wheelset. If $p_1$ is shorter than that relating to free curving then constrained curving takes place. For a truck with positively located wheelsets lacking any side play the directing arm of the leading wheelset is

$$p_1 = (a/2) + R\,c/a$$

where $a$ is the wheelbase, $R$ the curve radius and $c$ the total clearance between the two flanges of one wheelset and the adjoining railheads. The magnitude of $p_1$ locates the relevant friction force center $M_2$. A vertical from $M_2$ upwards to the $M$-curve locates the point 2 and a tangent from this supplies the points $A$ and $C$ on the lines extending vertically upwards from the truck axle centers. The points $A$ and $C$ permit the determination of the wheel directing forces $P_1$ and $P_2$ applied at the flanges of the outer leading and inner trailing wheels.

The force acting upon the leading wheel will be

$$P_1 = (AB/BD)\,2Qf_s$$

and that at the trailing wheel will be

$$P_2 = (CD/BD)\,2Qf_s.$$

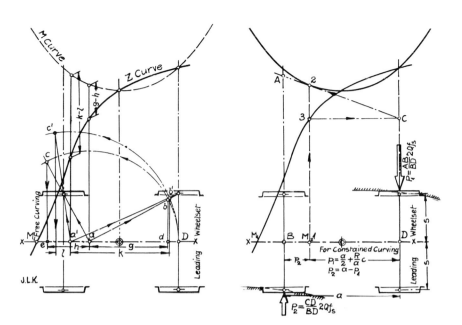

▲ The Z curve insures accuracy in the determination of flange forces and flange and tread wear due to constrained curving with outer leading and inner trailing wheel forced against the rails.

The use of the $M$ and $Z$ curves for the determination of the rail directing forces ▲ $P$ shown for the case of a 6' wheelbase standard gauge truck under conditions of constrained curving. With free curving $M$ is located behind the rear axle regardless of curve radius $R$. With constrained curving $M$ moves between the axles and closer to the kingpin with smaller $R$ values.

However some inaccuracy in these determinations could be encountered due to the difficulty of precise location of the tangent to the relatively flat $M$-curve. To overcome this the Z-curve was devised by Prof. Heumann. This is plotted by drawing circles from a number of arbitrarily chosen points a, a' etc. along the truck center line $x - x$, the radii being $aD$, $a'D$ etc. Next are drawn the wheel slide arms extending from $a,a'$, etc., through the wheel tread to rail contact points to the intersection with the corresponding circles at b and b', c and c', etc. The points e and c', b and b' etc. projected from these intersections on to the $x$-$x$ axis supply the distances $g = ad$, $h = ae$ etc., and the differences of these, $g - h$, etc., projected vertically down from the $M$-curve provide the points of the Z-line which is now plotted, point by point, to cross the $x$-$x$ axis at the friction force center for free curving at $M$ and the $M$-curve at the point corresponding to the kingpin location and again at a point in line with the leading wheelset. Once the $M$ and Z curves are to hand the $P_1$ and $P_2$ forces acting at the wheel flanges of a truck running at constrained conditions through a curve can be readily determined by determining the length of the relevant directing force arm $p_1$ which locates the friction force center $M_2$ at 1. A vertical projected from $M_2$ to the $M$-curve bisects the Z-curve at 3 and the $M$-curve at 2. A line from 3, parallel to the $x$-$x$ axis bisects the vertical from $D$ to the $M$-curve, this supplying $C$. A line from $C$ to 2, continued to $A$ locates the required tangent to the *M*-curve, thus locating both A and C. It is now readily possible to determine the magnitude of the forces acting at the flanges of both wheels guiding the truck through the curve as

$$P_1 = (AB/BD)\,2Qf_s$$

and

$$P_2 = (CD/DB)\,2Qf_s$$

as well as the flange wear data. With the coefficient of wheel to rail adhesion $f$ the tread wear can be ascertained as

$$\alpha_t = 2Qf\,q/Rr$$

where $q$ is the slide arm concerned while $f$ is generally assumed at 0.25.

This simple procedure permits an effective evaluation of the main factors influencing the forces and wheel wear encountered by trucks on their way through curves and the possible effectiveness of measures contemplated to insure increasingly effective operation. One way of assisting in this aim is to replace the prevailing standard tire profiles by the worn version as originated by Prof. Heumann. With these, the profile remains virtually unaltered in service, the truing up consisting of suitably turning down the flange tip as well as the outer tread section as grown with the tread wear without removing the valuable running and flange surface cold rolled and hardened in service. This as well as the change from the prevailing 60° flange angle to one of 68° to 70° was sponsored by Prof. Heumann to improve safety against derailment and reduce operating costs and both steps have now been implemented by many European railways.

The use of "loose" or individually driven wheels as with Tucson cars of 1916, Twin Coach demonstration four-wheelers of 1928 Lehigh Valley double truck car of 1931, the Montos four-wheeler of Essen and fifty Berlin trailers of 1928, it was intended to insure easy running through curves and prevent hunting motion at speed. As far as curve passage is concerned, individually rotating wheels eliminate the longitudinal slipping

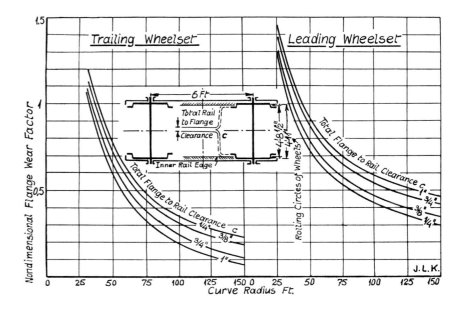

Flange-to-rail clearance is of great importance as far as wear in curves is concerned. Increased clearance increases wear at leading but reduces that at trailing wheels. With single end cars it would pay to reverse trucks from time to time.

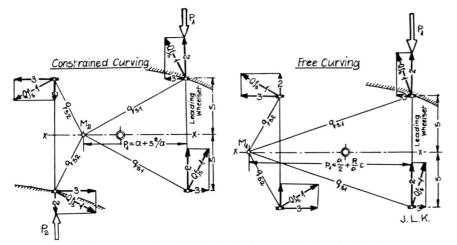

The forces acting on the wheels of a standard gauge, 6' wheelbase truck during its passage through curves can be readily appreciated once the location of the friction force center *M* is determined. Replacing standard wheelsets by loose wheels eliminates longitudinal slide resistance *3* thus reducing the motion opposing force from *1* to *2*.

resistance *3* so that the remaining lateral slip from *2* is left to replace the combined resistance *1* thus reducing the curve resistance by about ⅓. The resultant reduction in current consumption and wear will depend on curve radius and frequency and in most cases does not justify the required complications.

While with loose wheels the tendency of trucks to hunt would be checked, particularly at speeds in excess of about 75-100 mph they would be of little benefit at typical street railway speeds. Furthermore in a truck with loose wheels, a wheel running up against the rail would tend to stay that way until disturbed by an outside force. The required drive arrangement would be more complex, with all that this means as far as maintenance is concerned, while the slipping or spinning of one wheel would not be checked by the equalizing action of the other.

The use of trucks with self-steering wheelsets originated by the late Swiss engineer Roman Liechty has been resurrected. At the expense of a steering gear actuated by the rotation of the leading truck relative to the car body, the desired action seems achievable, but the problem remains how to prevent unwanted steering action from being initiated by truck hunting or body oscillation and how to do all this without demanding excessive exacting maintenance.

J. L. K.

# SOME FUNDAMENTALS OF TRUCK DESIGN

A railway car truck has three axes along and about which it can oscillate:

The vertical axis through the center of gravity of the spring-supported truck mass along which the truck can bounce up and down and rotate in the nosing mode;

The lateral axis rotation about which is known as pitching;

The longitudinal axis along which the truck may oscillate fore-and-aft, longitudinally or rotate roll fashion.

Oscillations in one plane or about one axis may combine with oscillations in another. Longitudinal ones may combine with pitching to produce rocking; combining with nosing will cause jerking. Lateral oscillations in conjunction with nosing cause hunting and when combined with rolling cause swaying. A combination of rolling and bouncing results in shimmy; bouncing and pitching together cause galloping. The main problems are bouncing, pitching and lateral oscillation.

Effective truck design copes with the frequency and amplitude of oscillation excited at track level and those imposed on the car body by damping. Riding quality acceptable to passengers drives good design.

Experience shows that accelerations faced by seated or standing passengers should not exceed the following values:

| | Excitation Frequency, Hz (cycles per second) | | | | | | | | | |
|---|---|---|---|---|---|---|---|---|---|---|
| | 1 | 2 | 3 | 4 | 5 | 6 | 7 | 8 | 9 | 10 |
| Acceleration, ft/sec² | | | | | | | | | | |
| Vertical plane | 2.6 | 2.1 | 1.8 | 1.6 | 1.6 | 1.6 | 1.7 | 2. | | 2.2 | 2.5 |
| Horizontal plane | 2.6 | 1.6 | 1.3 | 1.2 | 1.2 | 1.3 | 1.5 | 1.8 | 2.0 | 2.1 |

Note that passengers are more sensitive to oscillations that are horizontal (longitudinal or lateral) than to those that are vertical. Reduced sensitivity at lower frequencies as indicated by the higher acceleration tolerated is understandable since heart beat and walking pace as well as natural frequencies of certain organs approximate one per second. Effective design requires the knowledge of the excitation frequencies encountered in service. For example, vertical excitations, even over welded rails, originate at rail joints and also midway between them so that with a car running at 40 mph over 60′ rails excitation frequencies will be 1-2 Hz. In the lateral plane excitation frequencies depend on track gauge, wheel diameter, tire conicity and method of securing wheelsets in the truck frame.

With conventional axlebox to hornguide clearances, a wheelset has sufficient freedom to pursue a sinusoidal wave path down the track. With the modern practice of restraining wheelsets with the aid of links, radius arms or rubber suspensions, the two mutually interdependent wheelsets in a truck are forced to an elongated sinusoidal path which reduces the frequency of lateral excitation.

The effect of wheelset parameters on excitation frequency can be determined by an equation derived by Klingel in 1884, while the influence of axle restraint was determined by Heumann in 1940. As an example consider standard gauge wheelsets with 1:10, 1:20 and 1:40 treads. At 40 mph the excitation frequencies of the truck running on free wheels will be 1.77, 1.25 and 0.9 Hz with 27″ diameter free wheels, or 1.7, 1.2 and 0.84 Hz with 30″ wheels, these frequencies being directly proportional to the speed. Positively locating the axles in a 72″ wheelbase truck reduces these frequencies by a factor of about 1.6. However with some rubber suspensions it was found that the forces generated by the wheels overcame the restraining forces above about 25 mph so that the wheels followed the higher frequency path of the free assembly.

The North Shore Line and the other Chicago area Insull-controlled roads used cylindrical treads to eliminate the sinusoidal wheel path. However, with this, wheels may run with flanges rubbing against the rail while the tread will wear hollow thus reverting to rough running.

Next the designer strives for the suspension needed to insure that normal operating speeds will be below (subcritical) or above (supracritical) to the resonant (critical) speed at which the excitation and the natural vehicle frequencies of the vertical or lateral suspension elements coincide. With a 72″ wheelbase truck required to run at 30 mph the excitation frequency in the vertical plane would be about 0.7 and 0.35 cycles per sec. In this case it will be right to run in the subcritical range, with a spring system having a natural frequency above 1 Hz at a maximum of 40 mph. Here a total, static spring deflection of about 2.6″ at tare and 3″ at full load would result in vertical body oscillation frequencies of 1.95 and 1.8 Hz respectively. Using hydraulic snubbers with a damping factor of 0.25 the amplitude of the vertical body oscillations, at 40 mph would amount to about 1.2 times the wheel amplitude, increasing to about 1.3 at 60 mph.

The natural frequencies and damping values of vertical vehicle oscillation can be readily determined by slowly running off ¾″ wedges placed under all wheels. The impact of the car falling back on the rails excites the natural frequency while the damping factor is determined by the number of oscillations to rest. A damping factor of 0.25 should bring the oscillation to rest within 2½ cycles.

Somewhat similar considerations relate to the oscillations in the lateral plane. The body should be connected to the trucks with the aid of swing links or equivalent devices providing a not unduly rigid coupling. In the lateral plane the natural frequency of the assembly should be well above or well below the excitation frequencies likely to emanate from the truck at operationally important speeds. Thus with excitation at 30-40 mph in the order of 0.9-1.2 Hz with conventionally located wheelsets (or about 0.56-0.75 Hz with positively located wheelsets) with 12″ swing links inclined towards the outside, thus reducing the effective lengths to about 8″ and the natural frequency of lateral body oscillations to about 1.1 Hz, and with hydraulic damping to a factor of 0.4, the amplitude of body oscillations will be about 1.5 of the lateral wheel displacement. For the comfort of standing passengers the lateral acceleration running through curves should not exceed 3 ft/sec². This means that the corresponding bolster displacement will not exceed 10% of the effective swing line length. If this might exceed the available space, use must be made of suitable limiting devices.

Trucks are usually connected to the body with the aid of a kingpin located well above or below the center of gravity of the sprung truck mass. This may force the kingpin to impart unpleasant longitudinal oscillations to the car body. This, as well as possible locking of bolster vertically by the check plates when starting or stopping, can be mitigated by securing the bolster to the frame and the truck to the car body by suitably proportioned rubber-bushed links.

The design must deal with longitudinal forces equal to about three times the truck weight since such could be encountered in case of collision or derailment at speed. Safety considerations in case of derailment, switch-splitting, flange wear, and suppression of truck hunting also indicate that the resistance to truck rotation should be "not too little, not too much". Accordingly, truck torque should calculate within 0.03 to 0.05 times the truck wheelbase in feet and the load of one axle in tons.

Some designs are prone to derailment when leaving superelevated curves, with the outer rail falling away from under the wheel. To avoid this the wheel load under such circumstances should not fall below about 60-70% of the nominal value with 60° flange angles or 55-60% with 70° flange angles.

Prior to the PCC and other modern truck designs using air and rubber suspensions or systems of positive wheelset guidance, the peak of perfection was reached with type 39 E Maximum Traction as well as 76 E, 77 E, and 177 E equal-wheel trucks brought out by the J. G. Brill Co. between 1916 and 1926. Their slender frames permitted ready access to brake riggings. Bolster and axlebox springs were well in line with frame members thus eliminating undesirable torsional stresses. Long longitudinal laminated bolster springs reduced frame bending loads. Springs were placed widely apart permitting a soft suspension without causing underbody sway at the higher speeds. The number of bolster spring plates was kept to six or seven, this improving critical friction damping characteristics. The helical spring on top of the laminated elliptic was closed so that under two-thirds seated load, 75% of the total deflections are allocated to the bolster. These values are suitable for good riding qualities up to about 45 mph. Limiting axlebox spring deflection to 25% of the total prevents undue truck pitching oscillation and rough riding. Bolster guide links were somewhat short as to lateral displacement.

Altogether Brill trucks were outstanding in every way. There was virtually nothing wrong. Nothing matched them. It is only right and proper for transport museums to preserve these remarkable examples of ingenuity and exemplary engineering.

J. L. K.

## THE STEERING OF TRUCK WHEELSETS

This is the unusual story of steered axles as developed by the late (1981) Roman Liechty. His was a sad story. The idea of steered axles was started by his father, a Swiss Department of Transport inspector who published papers on steering of axles and articulated steam locomotives. Roman went on with it. Before World War II he founded in Neuchatel the "Compagnie Internationale d'Exploitation des Inventions Liechty pour Vehicules sur Rails", which worked in close accord with the SIG (Schweizerische Industrie Gesellschaft). About 1930 AEG tried to get the traction business going and with a car builder and Liechty produced a four axle articulated car a la Peter Witt. The end axles were rigid under the body sections but the two middle axles had pins toward the car center and could swing with the end ones via a flexible joint. Above 25 mph the ride was somewhat lively. Anyway nothing came of it.

Liechty turned to steerable axles, producing papers and finally getting Bern Loetschberg Simplon Railway and the Swiss Federal Railways interested in it. However while flange wear was reduced, the maintenance was too exacting.

Liechty did not give up. The Swiss Brown Boveri Company took him on, but since he was a bit of a pest as far as Swiss railways were concerned, BBC put him on electric drives for textile and paper machinery. It just about broke his heart since in his own time it was steered axles all the way. A big, heavy man, he seldom talked about anything else. Towards the end he spent most of his time organizing the railway side of the Technical High School library at Zurich. When I last saw him in 1978 at Aachen, he was in rather poor health but still happiest talking of steered axles. Currently UTDC, LT, and others have started this all over again.

Most European street railways were slow to drop their unshakable belief that four-wheelers augmented by one, two and sometimes three trailers carrying a total of some one hundred passengers and needing a crew of up to five was the efficient way of handling heavy city traffic. So stressed by literary, religious and political activists of all shades and denominations, faithfulness was viewed as a virtue to be taken seriously. Extended to street railway engineering and operation this had devastating results. Adherence to the four-wheeler led to the development of 36′ long cars on 12′ wheelbase trucks which in turn made it necessary to increase curve radii to at least 100′.

Use was also made of single axle trucks. Different designs were introduced in fairly large numbers, but they were not satisfactory as to riding qualities and maintenance demands. Most ended up with the wheelset frames rigidly connected by side members into four-wheel trucks. The use of six-wheelers with the outer, motored, wheelsets steered by a centrally located trailing wheelset as originally introduced by Robinson in 1889 and used in fairly large numbers, though scarcely successful, in Boston, was repeatedly tried in a number of variations, mostly of European origin, until for a while this became popular with a number of undertakings, most of all in Munich, in the form of a six-wheel design due to Jacob Buchli, General Manager of the Swiss Locomotive and Machine Works at Winterthur. However undue hunting at higher speeds or on

worn tracks caused by the small steering wheels led to disillusion and to the long overdue introduction of double truck cars, to start with in Italy and Switzerland, rapidly spreading to all European countries some forty-five to fifty years after they became popular in the U.S.A.

At the same time the general development of reliable equipment as well as the widespread use of dynamic braking in conjunction with holding disc brakes and the resultant reduction of wheel tread wear called for measures designed to reduce flange and rail wear in curves which gave most cause for concern. As shown by Prof. Heumann the latter is proportional to the friction between flange and rail, hence curve or flange lubrication, and the product of the force imposed upon the flange on its way through

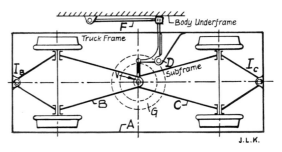

Early design of Liechty wheelset steered truck with the steered subframes actuated by levers operated by the truck rotation when entering or leaving a curve.

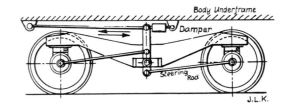

Liechty's early steering gear for trailer trucks was unduly responsive to hunting and lateral oscillations capable of actuating the steering thus adversely affecting the riding at speed.

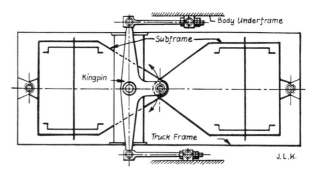

To prevent oscillations from affecting steering gear action Liechty devised the coupling of the steering gear to both sides of the body frame.

the curve and the angle at which the flange "attacks" the rail. With the wheel proceeding on its tread the point of contact of the outer leading wheel with the rail will move ahead, the distance covered increasing with the wheel diameter and the angle of attack. Since for a given curve radius the angle of flange-to-rail attack will increase with the wheelbase as well as with the total wheelset flange-to-rail clearance, the latter should be kept small. Thus with a 6 ft. wheelbase truck, running through 100-300 ft. radius curves, reducing the total clearance from 1" to ¾", ½", and ¼" would reduce flange wear from unity to 0.9, 0.7, and 0.55 respectively.

Flange and rail wear can be further reduced by reducing the angle of attack with the aid of wheelset steering which attracted the early attention of inventors, the first relevant U.S. patent being granted to Thomas H. Cowley on January 12, 1913 under Nr 1,051,214 though without leading to a practical application. The actual development of workable power and trailing trucks for interurban and main line cars was achieved by Roman Liechty, who devoted most of his life to the perfection of his ideas. His designs may be explained by reference to car 787, later 721, built in 1935 for the Loetschberg railway which in addition to its 63.5 mile main line from Thun to Brig operates a number of lines out of Bern and Spiez, the total network embracing some 145 miles. The 60', 24t, 300 hp car was designed for a top speed of 56 mph with the car body supported on the truck by the ring $G$, the wheelbase from the outer, trailing, axle to this amounting to 55½" as compared with 78¾" for the motored one. The main truck frame $A$ is connected by the pins $I_B$ and $I_C$ with the wheelset frames $B$ and $C$ which carry the motor and brake gear and are permitted to articulate about the center at $V$. Upon entering a curve the truck frame $A$ will turn relative to the car body while the frames $B$ and $C$ will be steered by the rectangular lever located in the truck at $D$, the motion being imposed by the lever $F$ connected to the underframe.

According to Prof. Heumann: "The, by no means small, force required to steer the four wheelsets of a double truck vehicle must be provided by the outer leading wheel of the leading truck entering the curve. The design is also rather sensitive to any backlash in the steering system," while the wheelsets must be maintained at right angle to the track on straight sections.

While the results obtained with this car met the expectations it was unable to meet the needs of the steadily growing traffic. It was sold to the 2.7 mile Oensingen-Balsthal Railway whose 820' radius curves did not justify the use of steered wheelsets so the Liechty trucks were replaced in 1958 by conventional ones. Articulated power cars were obtained by the Loetschberg Railway in 1939. The 133' long, 80t, 900 hp, 75 mph cars incorporated Liechty power and trailing trucks, the middle one being arranged so that car separation could be accomplished within 20 minutes. With financial assistance from the cities concerned the Swiss Federal Railways acquired in 1938 power car number 701 for operation between La Chaux de Fonds, Neuchatel, Bienne and LeLocle. This 72' long, 44t, 600 hp Jura Arrow was provided with 141½" wheelbase Liechty trucks and after service on various lines, wound up at Rohrschach harbor where it served until fairly recently.

In Germany 138" wheelbase Liechty trucks were used under the 78'6" long diesel-mechanical rail car acquired in 1941 by the 7.7 mile Tegernsee Railway which had operating rights over the 37 miles to Munich reached in one hour flat. The car was in service until 1966. Although 650-1000 ft. radius curves claimed only some 6% of the line, the railway claimed that the Liechty trucks doubled the tire life. In the case of trailer cars on the Berchtesgaden-Koenigssee line, the Liechty arrangement reduced the angle of attack from 0.9° to 0.3° and was said to increase rail life 1½ fold.

Trucks with steered wheelsets are more complex, require more exacting upkeep and are more costly than conventional versions. However this should not detract from Liechty's design achievements which, particularly in more recent times, have been resurrected by a number of designers and organizations. Some of these proposals bring to mind the comment made in 1865 by W. H. Russel in connection with laying of the first transatlantic cable: "When the testimony on which men's reputations, as finders or makers rest, is critically examined, a suspicion is often generated that there have been many Vespuccis in the world who have given names to places they never found,

and taken or received credit for what they never did". Liechty was the true originator of the working version of the steered wheelset truck; hopefully there will be no Vespucci to claim being first.

J. L. K.

# RUNNING THROUGH CURVES

In some recent fascinating histories of the interurbans reference is made to the cars' inability to negotiate the curves encountered in narrow city streets or the loops at the city terminals. Just what caused the problem isn't often made clear. Was the trouble caused by a wrong track layout, faulty gauging or wrong truck-body clearances restricting the truck from turning within the limits set by underframe members, or brake rigging or both?

One would hope that the possibility of such calamities would have been studied and avoided in the design stage. With the aid of graphical investigations such limitations could all be checked by simulation. For years this was done by a scaled down drawing accurately laid out on a big drawing table using beam compass or pre-cut railroad curves. Today it can be quickly done with computer-aided graphics equipment.

The time and effort required by cumbersome investigation was not necessarily commensurate with the degree of accuracy required, particularly when it came to constrained running of a truck through narrow curves bereft of gauge widening. Constrained curve running signifies that the truck runs through the curve with the outer leading wheel up against the outer rail and the inner trailing wheel up against the inner rail, as compared to free curving, in which only the outer leading wheel proceeds with the flange running against the rail and the rear wheelset moves freely within the channel offered by the track layout and the flange profile. Actually, *constrained* curving is not necessarily to be avoided by special attention to car and track design. The guiding forces acting on the outer leading and the inner trailing wheels, though causing flange and rail wear, can distribute this rather than heap it all on the outer leading wheel flange. Thus while the total amount of wear might be increased it may not require flange recontouring as frequently as when the outer leading wheel is expected to do all the work alone. Of course, this is certainly no justification for inadequate design effort.

Whether the truck is running free or constrained through a curve depends on whether its friction force center is located sufficiently to the rear of the leading wheelset, behind the trailing one (regardless of whether the latter is driven or not). In the case of free curving this distance should be at least

$$p_{fr} = a + s^2/a$$

to the rear of the leading wheelset or the curve radius at least

$$R = a^2/c$$

where $a$ is the truck wheelbase and $s$ half the distance between the rolling circles of the wheelset and $c$ the total flange-to-rail clearance. Thus for $a = 72"$ and $s = 29½"$ for standard gauge, $p_{fr} = 84"$.

For the truck moving through an $R = 300'$ curve and the total flange to rail clearance $c = ½"$ the friction force center distance behind the leading wheelset will be given as

$$p_1 = (a/2) + (Rc/a) = 61"$$

so that, with $p_a$ smaller than $p_{fr}$, constrained curving will occur. However it would be counterproductive to increase $c$ to move $p_1$ further back since this would increase the angle at which the leading outer wheel flange would attack the rail, increasing flange and rail wear. A quick and convenient way of determining vehicle location in a curve was devised by Prof. Rudolf Vogel (1886-1974) as the result of a wound to an arm in World War I. This restricted his use of the beam compass when dealing with track layouts which became his major preoccupation. To solve his personal problem he hit upon the idea of converting the circular curve layout of his investigations into a parabolic one, the resultant error being a fraction of 1%. In this manner it became possible to carry out the relevant investigations to a much smaller scale while insuring exact determination of the required dimensions, given the relevant data. The method is based on shrinking both vehicle and track width, so that in the plan view the former is represented by its center line and the latter by two lines separated by the width $c$ of the entire clearance between both flanges of one wheelset and the inner edges of the two rails. The vehicle length is usually reduced to the scale of 1:50 or 1:100, depending on vehicle size and that of the available sheet. The value of $c$ and of the vertical distances of the curve from the horizontal reference line can be full or half-size, again depending on the available paper size. The plot of the curve is based on the conversion of the circle representing the relevant curve into a parabola where the distance $y$ vertically below the reference line is calculated as

$$y = x^2/2R$$

where $x$ is the distance along the horizontal reference and $R$ is the curve radius. In a horizontal scale of 1:100, an actual length of $100''$ is represented by a scale $1''$ from $0$ along the $x$-axis. For a curve radius $R = 300'$, the scale location of the track at a point below the $x$-axis becomes $y = 0.116'$.

Similarly, for $x = 16'8''$ is $5.55''$ down, and so on. In this manner, a parabolic simulation is developed for the outer rail, shown on a $x$-scale of 1:100 and a $y$-scale of 1:1. The magnitude of the rail clearance is assumed at $c = \frac{1}{2}''$ and the inner rail plotted at this distance $c$ the way down. In Vogel's simulation, all dimensions must be plotted and read off only horizontally along the $x$-axis and vertically along the $y$-axis and never along any inclined line. Plotting is simplified by using metric dimensions.

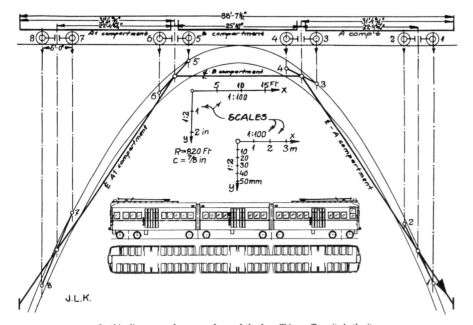

In this diagram performance of one of the four Chicago Transit Authority articulated cars in an 820' radius curve is plotted in accordance with Vogel's method of curve running investigation.

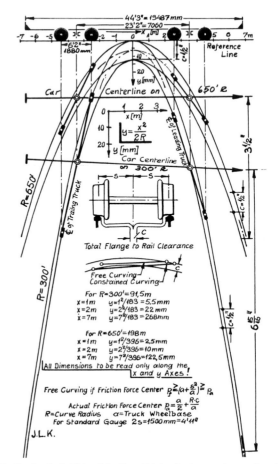

The Vogel method of determining the vehicle location in curves is accurate and conserves space. This example is for the C & LE Red Devil in 300 and 650' radius curves.

As an example consider the passage of a Cincinnati and Lake Erie Railroad "Red Devil" high-speed car through curves of 300' and 650' radius, the plot being carried out on a letter sized sheet. The car is drawn on a scale of 1:100 along the reference line of the $x$-axis while the curve rail lines are plotted to a scale of 1:1 along the $y$-axis. The wheel centers are projected down to their location with the track channel $c$, both trucks running freely through the 650' curve but forced into restrained curving through the 300' curve. The plot shows that in the 300' curve the front end of the car swings about 7" from the track center (as compared with 3½" in the 650' curve) while the rear wheel-sets swing out about 1¾" (and $^{13}/_{16}$" respectively). The angle of the truck in the curve can be determined as well although paying attention to the scales involved. Thus the leading wheelset of the rear truck running through the 300' curve assumes an angle of 2°-45'.

Once the basic idea behind the Vogel method becomes clear it can be applied for single or articulated cars. The results are of considerable assistance in determining the mechanics of curve-running.

J.L.K.

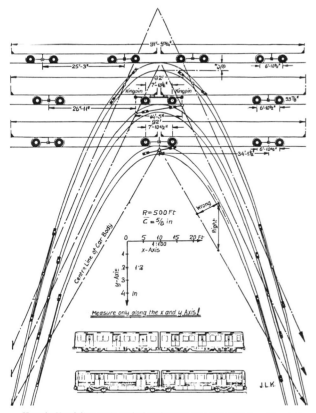

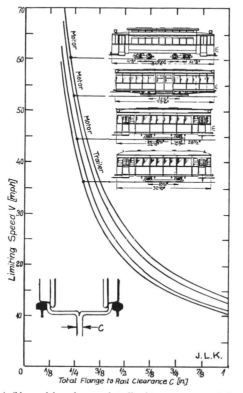

Here the Vogel diagram is applied to the 1958 cars of the Hamburg Elevated. Running through 500' radius curves at a total flange to rail clearance of ⅝" (worn conditions) would cause the adjoining car ends to swing about 4½", the outer ends some 4¼" and shift the body about 2" out of track center line. In a 1966 model the adjoining bodies were supported by springs mounted from kingpins on the outer ends of the truck frame. The relevant plot shows that apart from the car ends the bodies swing out to a lesser extent than would either two close-coupled cars or conventional articulation.

Permissible speed depends on comfort offered to passengers was indicated by forces generated by the hunting oscillations of speeding cars. Apart from forces determined by vehicle inertia and vibrational characteristics, acceptable speeds are influenced by the flange-to-rail clearance values as shown for a number of prewar streetcar types. Their importance is confirmed by the tightening of the relevant values by many railroads. On street railways $c$ varies from $\frac{3}{16}$" new to 1" worn as compared with $\frac{3}{8}$" to $1\frac{9}{16}$" on rapid transit lines. To maintain tire shape and flange-to-rail clearance between overhauls, the worn tire profile pioneered by Prof. Heumann is used to assure one point of contact.

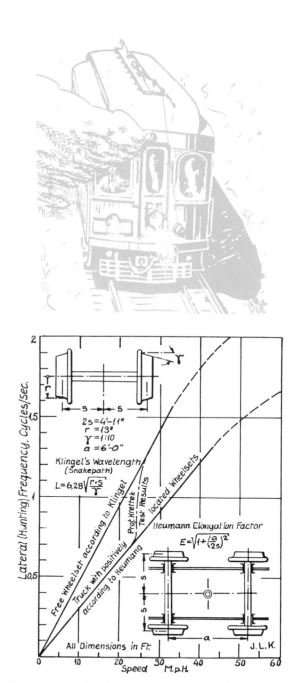

The frequency of the truck hunting oscillations depend on wheel size, gauge, tread conicity and, with positively located wheelsets, on the truck wheelbase.

*Please refer to the text on page 24,*
*THE SNAKEPATH OF THE INTERURBAN*

125

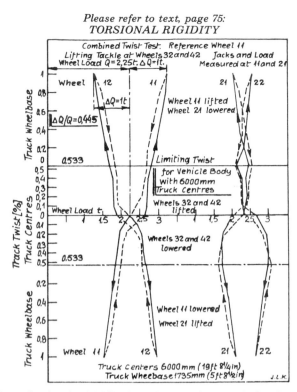

*Please refer to text, page 75:*
## TORSIONAL RIGIDITY

Combined Twist Test: Reference Wheel 11
Lifting Tackle at Wheels 32 and 42   Jacks and Load
Wheel Load Q=2,25t. ΔQ=1t      Measured at 11 and 21

Truck Centers 6000mm (19ft 8¼in)
Truck Wheebase 1735mm (5ft 8½in)

The results of torsional rigidity determinations relating to wheel 11 show that for the vehicle concerned *delta Q/Q* does not exceed the acceptable limit. The direction of the loads at wheels 21 and 22 are reversed due to the test conditions.

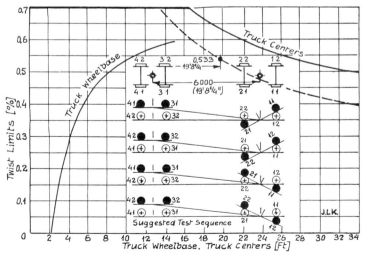

The track twist faced by European railways must be met without excessively reducing wheel load. Prevailing conditions resulted in two limits for truck center distances. Truck twisted simultaneously with vehicle body to face possible "potholes" in track.

## TABLE OF CONTENTS

°Standard two-letter abbreviations designated by the U.S. Post Office are used throughout this book.

# BIBLIOGRAPHY

The broad general base of reference for the captions and descriptions as well as the essays contained in this book are the publications of the trade press of the electric railway industry for the period from the 1880s to the present. Another, and equally valuable source, was the collective observations and records of individual historians and enthusiasts who are generally included in the acknowledgments at the beginning of this book. The most significant of these are listed below.

For brevity, in the case of those many references drawn from parts of a continuing series of publications from a single source, only that source is referenced and not the individual issues used.

Listings are alphabetical by author, except where no author was identified the listing is by title.

AMERICAN PUBLIC TRANSIT ASSOCIATION
Transit Passenger Vehicle Inventory

AMERICAN STREET RAILWAY INVESTMENTS
The Street Railway Publishing Co., 1899

BRILL MAGAZINE, catalogs, data sheets and drawings, 1895-1945

Central Electric Railfans' Association,
Bulletins 1-125, 1938-1986

Chandler (Allison) and Maguire (Stephen D.)
WHEN OKLAHOMA TOOK THE TROLLEY
Interurbans Press, 1980

Cincinnati Car Company
Correspondence 1932-1938
Other records as compiled by
Dr. Harold E. Cox

Culp, Edwin D.
STATIONS WEST, OREGON RAILWAYS
The Caxton Printers, Ltd., 1972

Cummings, O. R.
ATLANTIC SHORE LINE RY.
Transportation, Connecticut Valley
Chapter, Nat'l. Ry. Hist. Soc., 1950
ATLANTIC SHORE TROLLEYS
New England Electric Railway Historical
Society, Inc., 1966

DeGraw, Ronald
THE RED ARROW
Ronald DeGraw, 1972
RED ARROW, THE FIRST HUNDRED YEARS
Interurban Press, 1985

Demoro, Harre
ELECTRIC RAILWAY PIONEER
Interurban Press, 1983
THE KEY ROUTE, Parts 1 and 2
Interurban Press, 1985
CALIFORNIA'S ELECTRIC RAILWAYS
Interurban Press, 1986

Dodge, John W.
ELECTRIC RAILROADING IN CENTRAL
CALIFORNIA
Pacific Railway Journal, 1956

Dubin, Arthur Detmers
SOME CLASSIC TRAINS
Kalmbach Publishing, 1964
MORE CLASSIC TRAINS
Kalmbach Publishing, 1974

ECONOMIST, THE, Street Railway Supplement
The Economist Publishing Co., 1896

THE ELECTRIC RAILWAY NUMBER,
Cassier's Magazine
The Cassier Magazine Co., 1899

Fetters (Thomas) and Swanson (Peter W., Jr.)
PIEDMONT & NORTHERN RAILWAY
Golden West Books, 1974

Forsyth, Harold D.
NEW YORK CENTRAL LINES, Description of
Electric and Diesel-El. Locomotives
Published by the author, 1944

Garma Franco, Francisco
RAILROADS IN MEXICO, Vols. I and II
Sundance Books, 1985 and 1988

GENERAL ELECTRIC REVIEW, also GE catalogs,
data sheets and drawings
General Electric Company, 1895-1965

HEADLIGHTS and other publications
Electric Railroaders' Association, 1938 to date

Heseltine (Charles D.) and Robertson (Edwin B.)
AROOSTOOK VALLEY RAILROAD
Robertson Books, 1987

Hilton (George W.) and Due (John F.)
THE ELECTRIC INTERURBAN RAILWAY
IN AMERICA
Stanford University Press, 1960

Holley, Noel T.
THE MILWAUKEE ELECTRICS
N. J. International Inc., 1987

Horine (J. W.) and Ogden (H. S.)
THE PENNSYLVANIA R.R. CLASS GG-1
ELECTRIC LOCOMOTIVE
American Institute of Electrical Engineers
Transaction paper, 1959

Hutchinson, W. A.
AC ELECTRIC MOTORS FOR
PENNSYLVANIA R.R.
(Correspondence documenting history and
development in period 1915-1948)
Westinghouse Electric & Manufacturing Co., 1948

Jackson, Kenneth G.
APPLE COUNTRY INTERURBAN
Golden West Books, 1979

Keenan, Jack
CINCINNATI & LAKE ERIE RAILROAD
Golden West Books, 1974

Lind, A.R.
FROM HORSES TO STREAMLINERS
Transport History Press, 1978

Long Island Rail Road
PASSENGER CAR CLASSIFICATION BOOK
Long Island R.R., 1973

McGRAW ELECTRIC RAILWAY DIRECTORY
McGRAW ELECTRIC RAILWAY MANUAL
McGraw-Hill Publishing Co., 1899-1931

MASS TRANSPORTATION
MASS TRANSPORTATION DIRECTORY
ELECTRIC TRACTION (Magazine)
Kenfield-Davis Publishing Company, 1910-1945

Middleton, William D.
THE INTERURBAN ERA
Kalmbach Publishing, 1961
NORTH SHORE
Golden West Books, 1964
TRACTION CLASSICS, Vols 1-2-3
Golden West Books, 1963-1983-1985
WHEN THE STEAM ROADS ELECTRIFIED
Kalmbach Publishing 1974
THE TIME OF THE TROLLEY
Golden West Books, 1987

Mutschler (Charles V.) and Parent (Clyde L.)
SPOKANE'S STREET RAILWAYS
Inland Empire Railway Historical Soc., 1987

New York Central Railroad
Operating Timetables, var. divisions and dates

New York New Haven & Hartford Railroad
DESCRIPTION OF NYNH&HRR ELECTRIC
LOCOMOTIVES, 1931

NYNH&HRR ELECTRIC LOCOMOTIVE & M.U.
CAR DIAGRAM BOOK
NYNH&HRR Technical Info. Assoc. Inc.,
Ca 1973

Olson, Russell L.
THE ELECTRIC RAILWAYS OF MINNESOTA
Minnesota Transportation Museum, Inc., 1976

Pennsylvania Railroad
Electric Locomotive Diagram Book, 1930-1960

Railway Age (Magazine)
Various issues and dates

Railroad (Magazine)
Various issues and dates

Rowsome (Frank) and Maguire (Stephen D.)
TROLLEY CAR TREASURY
McGraw-Hill, 1956

Sacramento Northern Railway
Operating timetables and other data, 1931-1940

St. Louis Car Company
Catalogs, brochures and drawings, 1900-1965

Shaw, Donald E. (See TRANSPORTATION)

Smith, Vernon L.
ONE MAN'S LOCOMOTIVES
Trans-Anglo Books, 1987

Stindt (Fred A.) and Dunscomb (Guy L.)
THE NORTHWESTERN PACIFIC R.R.
Stindt and Dunscomb, 1964

Swett, Ira L.
PACIFIC ELECTRIC RAILWAY, Cars of,
Lines of
SACRAMENTO NORTHERN RY., Cars of,
Lines of
Interurbans, 1957-1966

TRANSIT JOURNAL
ELECTRIC RAILWAY JOURNAL
STREET RAILWAY JOURNAL
McGraw-Hill Publ. Co., 1899-1942

TRANSPORTATION (Magazine, various issues)
Connecticut Valley Chapter
National Railway Historical Society, 1945-1959

WESTINGHOUSE ELECTRIC &
MANUFACTURING CO.,
Bulletins, publications, catalogs and drawings,
1899-1965

Wagner (Richard M.) and Wagner (Birdella)
CURVED SIDE CARS BUILT BY THE
CINCINNATI CAR COMPANY    1965
TROLLEY TALK, various issues and dates

Walker, Jim
KEY SYSTEM ALBUM
Interurbans Press, 1978

Wood (Charles R.) and Wood (Dorothy M.)
MILWAUKEE ROAD WEST
Superior Publishing Company, 1972

Young, (Andrew D.) and Provenzo (Eugene F., Jr.)
ST. LOUIS CAR COMPANY
Howell-North Books, 1978

## INDEX A — Personalities

**INDEX B — Locations: Cities, states, provinces, countries, lakes, rivers, etc. Post Office Standard abbreviations are used to designate states in U.S.A.**

**INDEX C — Companies, Publications, Schools**

## INDEX D — General

ERRATA

| Page | Column | Paragraph | Line | Should read |
|------|--------|-----------|------|-------------|
| 24 | left | 2 | 7 | ... Württemberg.. |
| 24 | right | 4 | 4 | f = 3.14 Hz$\sqrt{1/L}$ |
| 123 | left | 6 | 12 | ..."Jura Arrow"... |
| 123 | right | 5 | 7 | R = $a^2/2c$ |
| 124 | left | 2 | 1 | Similarly, for $\underline{x}$ = 16'8", $\underline{y}$ is 5,55" down .. |
| 128 | right | Index A | | Add: Cummings, O.R. "Dick" |
| 128-129 | For additional contributors, please refer to listing on page 5 | | | |
| 129 | left | Index A | 2 | Add: 4, .. |
| 129 | left | Index A | | Add: Peterson, Elaine L. |
| 133 | left | Index C | 5 | ... Gesellschaft), .. |
| 133 | left | Index C | 23 | Add: ... 53, .. |

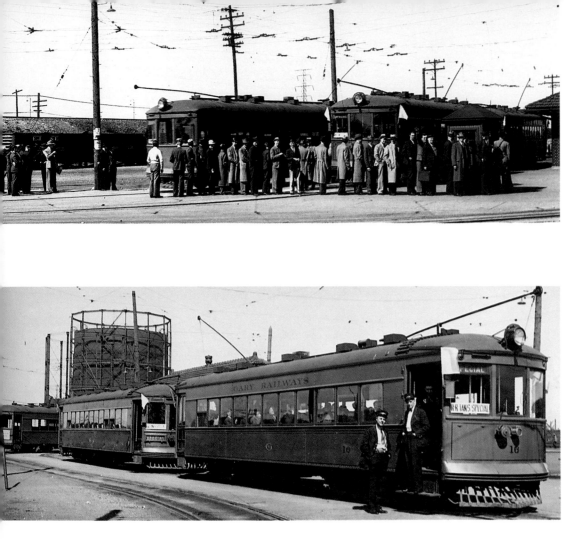

SPECIAL SUPPLEMENT
commemorating the
golden anniversary of the

# Central
# Electric
# Railfans'
# Association

# 1938-1988

by Norman Carlson

Almost 600 people participated in the celebration of CERA's golden anniversary held in Chicago over the Memorial Day weekend in 1988. The festivities began on Friday, May 27 with registration and a general membership meeting at the Hyatt Regency Chicago. With over 525 in attendance, the meeting set an all-time record for CERA and probably was the largest electric railfan gathering in the world.

Featured speaker was noted historian and author, William D. Middleton. Bill presented a fifty-year history of street car, interurban, rapid transit and main line electric railroad operations in the United States, illustrated by photographs from his vast collection. It is planned that this milestone presentation will be published as a CERA bulletin so that all members and friends of CERA may enjoy it.

CERA President Walter R. Keevil recognized founding members Frank E. Butts, Bernard L. "Barney" Stone and George "GK" Krambles. Frank was called to the podium and recalled how CERA had evolved from the May 1, 1938 inspection trip of the Gary Railways Valparaiso line which Frank had planned. He had even found an unissued ticket for that event and presented it to the meeting moderator.

A letter of greeting was read from Barney Stone, who for the first time was missing one of the five-year CERA anniversary celebrations.

Norm Carlson then told how, back in 1936 George Krambles had been hired as an engineer-trainee for Indiana Railroad by Louis Rappaport, General Auditor. Rappaport, who had come to IR from the South Shore Line, in addition to his financial responsibilities served as Agent for Receiver, de facto equivalent of chief operating officer. Encountering George in the trainshed at Traction Terminal at the end of only his second day's work, Rappaport politely inquired how things were going and whether there was anything he could do to help. GK brashly suggested that a card pass would facilitate familiarization with the property, but was told that the practice was to issue a trip pass after one year, a division pass after five and a system pass after 25! Nevertheless, next day's mail included a system pass and it goes without saying it was gratefully, but intensively used.

## DR. RIDLEY'S MESSAGE:

As the leader of Britain's Light Rail Transit Association and Chairman and Managing Director of London Underground Ltd, Dr. Tony Ridley had been an outstanding choice for guest speaker at the CERA Golden Anniversary banquet of May 28, 1988. When unforeseen circumstances upset this plan, Dr. Ridley graciously forwarded the following brief remarks in the form of an audio tape which received a well-earned accolade when played at the dinner:

"Hello, Chicago! This is Tony Ridley in London. I'm speaking as the President of the Light Rail Transit Association and sending very best wishes to the Central Electric Railfans' Association at the celebration of your 50th Anniversary.

"As you know, I had originally hoped to join you in Chicago to share in the celebration. I very much regret that circumstances have made it impossible for that to happen and that I cannot be with you in person to take part on your happy occasion.

"However, I was determined that I should in some way or other be able to send both my personal congratulations and those of the LRTA to you all. Both the CERA and LRTA were founded in the same era and both organizations have a great deal in common. Over the years, contacts between members of the two associations have grown in closeness, respect and affection, and naturally led to the formal affiliation that now happily exists.

"What members of the LRTA have particularly admired in your Association have been your bulletins—professional and comprehensive documents which faithfully and reliably chronical the development of electric rail traction in North America.

"The completion of fifty years in a condition of strength and continued growth is a considerable achievement and a milestone worthy of celebration. I wish you continued success as you progress toward your centenary and I hope that your anniversary weekend is most enjoyable for all concerned.

"Finally, if I may give a personal message, I would like to send very best wishes from all of his friends and fans in the U.K. to George Krambles.

"Thank you!"

Some early tickets and membership passes.

Carlson went on to say that today there is another Indiana Rail Road and it too operates out of Indianapolis; one of the new regional railroads. The current property spells the "railroad" of its name in two words to stay clear of corporate filings still in existence of the "Railroad." Through the courtesy of MCERA Thomas G. Hoback, President and Chief Executive Officer of The Indiana Rail Road, Norm Carlson, auditor of today's I R R was granted the privilege of presenting GK a pass "between all stations." GK now need only wait for that first passenger train, but in the meantime he is obviously the only person to have been a granted a pass on both railroads of this name.

Walt Keevil introduced each of the members of the arrangement committee and briefly told the special assignments they had in putting the event together; more about this later in this report.

CERA's first directors, from the left, Charles H. Brady, Charles A. Brown, George Krambles, Wallace M. Rogers and Bernard L. Stone.

Attention was especially called to the work of Max Zink, past CERA director and longtime cartographic specialist. Every CERA member has benefitted from Max' work. Unfortunately, he was unable to be with us to receive the plaque prepared in recognition of his efforts. The text of the presentation to Max follows:

Today we'd like to recognize a long-time CERA volunteer . . . in fact, CERA's most senior volunteer in point of continuous service. Maximillian A. Zink made his first appearance in the 1953 CERA bulletin and since 1955 he's worked continuously in the CERA publication program. In 33 years, I don't believe he's ever been away from the CERA workroom for more than a couple of months. He's now creating the first ever detailed track map of Indiana Railroad System for an upcoming book. And if you know Max, you know his maps are meticulously crafted works of art! . . .

Max is MCERA #283, dating back to July 9, 1941, but his standing as a railfan is much longer. He remembers when the Lawrence Avenue streetcar in Chicago was so far "out in the country" that it needed only two cars. And those were little single-truckers. Today it takes thirteen buses for the equivalent service.

I'm sure some other people in this room have ridden the Chicago & Joliet Electric Railway, but I doubt that anyone else rode a single-truck car on the Lyons branch. Now you may know how a single-trucker bounced along as if it's going to leave the track at the next rail joint. And you may even know that the Lyons line ran right alongside a deep stone quarry. Put that together and you'll know Max had a memorable trolley adventure!

Max might also be the only person in this room who rode the wooden cars of the Chicago Lake Shore & South Bend Railway . . . the "old, old" South Shore Lines cars . . . on field trips of his geology class at Chicago's Senn High School.

Later Max received his engineering degree from Armour Institute of Technology, now part of the Illinois Institute of Technology, and served his professional career in building design for the Illinois Bell Telephone Company.

They say that the reward for good work is the opportunity to do some more work. Max has done great work for CERA for a third of a century, so . . . we're looking forward to great maps in many more CERA bulletins. Your Board of Directors is pleased to recognize Max Zink, a richly deserved honor.

Dawn came on Saturday, May 28, with a few clouds that quickly dissipated into a clear and sunny day. Our trip on the Chicago South Shore & South Bend Railroad began with specially reserved cars attached to the rear of a scheduled train as far as Michigan City. There, the participants were divided into small groups for tours of the shops, conducted by senior executives of the South Shore Line. In a memorable story told by one member, in noting that his guide seemed very knowledgeable, not only of the shop, but of the whole railroad, asked him what his position was with the railroad. The reply: "I am the President." Yes, MCERA Tim Jorgensen, who has spoken at a CERA meeting, was one of the tour guides most happy to show off South Shore's facilities.

Following a family style luncheon, the group left Michigan City on a chartered train that made a high-speed non-stop run to South Bend. It then changed ends quickly to return east to Olive siding, where it met with a regular train. This was the first of many photo stops. Not only did the weather cooperate, but the adjacent Conrail main line managed to provide passing freight trains during the Olive and later Wagner photo stops. Return to Chicago was just in time to clean up and get dressed for the banquet of Saturday evening.

Hotel staff outdid themselves to provide a pleasant get-acquainted cocktail hour followed by sumptuous roast beef or salmon dinners. Then for

Directors Max Zink and Frank Misek strive to improve productivity in the preparation of Bulletin 99 in November 1955.

the evening's program. Due to priority issues at home, our intended guest of honor, Dr. Tony M. Ridley, Chairman and Managing Director, London Underground Limited, could not be with us. However, his taped message on behalf of Britain's Light Rail Transit Association was presented (see Box). Francis J. Goldsmith, Jr. then extended good wishes from the Electric Railroaders' Association. Dr. Richard L. Allman on behalf of the East Penn Traction Club transmitted a great collection of historic photos by David H. Cope along with greetings. Two South American groups, the Uruguayan Railfans Association (AUAR) and the (Inter-) American Rail and Electric Traction Fans Federation (FADARTE), both headquartered in Montevideo, sent messages, received with much pride, acknowledging the inspiration they had received from the example of CERA. A final preliminary was the introduction of the first 50 members (MCERA), a majority of whom remain active.

This brought us to the evening's featured speaker, MCERA #1, George Krambles. GK served the Chicago transit system for 43 years, rising from engineer/clerk to Executive Director before retirement. He's served CERA even longer . . . more than 50 years now, currently being in responsible charge of editing this very publication, CERA Bulletin 126, "A Rainbow of Traction." Krambles' talk recalled the history of CERA, illustrating with pictures of CERA personalities and activities over the years, much to the delight of the audience. There was many a laugh and a few tears as we

CTA's heritage train 4271-4272 approaches Dempster station on Skokie Swift meeting supplementary train of rehabbed PCC type.

CERA's Krambles discusses details of operation with French visitors while traversing CTA's Dan Ryan line.

—*Donald R. Kaplan photos*

reviewed some highlights of early meetings and trips that were operated when a now-departed generation of electric railways was flourishing.

Roads like the North Shore Line, Aurora-Elgin, South Shore Line, Chicago Rapid Transit, Waterloo Cedar Falls & Northern, Crandic, Illinois Terminal, Illinois Central, Indiana Railroad and Texas Electric truly extended themselves to welcome CERA members when they came on inspection trips. A sort of rivalry even developed between the North Shore and South Shore. For some early meetings, the former provided a coach and dining car parked in a sidetrack at Wilson Avenue where homebound commuters could stare in envy. On one trip the South Shore, then no longer having a serviceable dining car, nevertheless stripped the seats from coach 35 and installed a stand-up lunch counter for CERA's trip day. Krambles also reminded us of many members who have risen to key decision-making positions in the transit and railroad industry, where their broad interest and accurate knowledge of its history and technology have well served the public.

On Sunday, May 29, the sun was up bright and early and so were the participants, who were soon off on an all-day tour of Chicago Transit Authority's rapid transit lines, using three sets of equipment. Because of heavy construction work on the Ravenswood line at Merchandise Mart station which had to be done on the three-day weekend, some tricky routing had to be followed to interconnect the north, west and central parts of the day's itinerary. Among the benefits that sprang from this was a non-stop ride that covered the 5-mile State Street subway in slightly over eight minutes.

The train for most of the day consisted of six 6000-series cars in the current platinum mist paint scheme. During the afternoon the 300 participants separated into three sub-groups to ride on the preserved heritage train (cars 4271-4272) between Fullerton and Dempster, Skokie Swift. For the portion over the Swift, a train of recently rehabilitated PCC cars assigned to that line supplemented the heritage train. CTA crews and supervision outdid themselves to accommodate the group. Special thanks

Chicago Surface Lines 1374, designed by St. Louis Car in 1904, now faithfully restored under the direction of Frank Sirinek, bursts through commemorative banner to begin its renaissance as a working display at Illinois Railway Museum.

Noted author Bill Middleton, featured speaker at the general meeting, poses with the 1374; Frank Sirinek at controls.

—*Photos: Bill Hoffman, Norm Carlson*

go to CERA President Walt Keevil (CTA Superintendent, Electrical Vehicle Design) who worked with CTA's Transportation Department on a last minute basis to develop the very complex schedule needed to avoid the construction work and yet accomplish the goals of our trip.

Sunday evening was free and after a long hot day, participants eagerly departed for dinner and relaxation on an individual basis. Each registrant had been provided with a "goodies package" containing, among other things, suggested self-guided tours to restaurants in various parts of the Chicago area. The thrust of these tours, which were developed by CERA past-director Roy Benedict, was to ride out on one line, perhaps even a Metra commuter line, then return on another. Also included in the registration package was a CTA pass good on any rapid transit or bus line, the cost of which had been included in the registration fee. This pass, modeled after a one-day pass issued when Pope John Paul II visited Chicago in 1979, was developed especially for CERA by the CTA, who have decided, as a permanent marketing tool, to make available similar three-, five- or seven-day revenue passes to groups of 25 or more visiting Chicago for conventions.

On Monday, May 30, for the third day in a row the sun shone brightly when the group assembled for a complimentary breakfast before boarding charter coaches for the trip to visit the two outstanding railway museums just west of Chicago. Upon arrival at the Illinois Railway Museum at Union a group photo was taken using an antique 360° panoramic camera. A hokey tradition of the old days was followed with MCERA Dennis Furbush appearing at both ends of the same view. Then followed train riding and

picture taking of the great variety of equipment this museum has lovingly restored, a bit slowed perhaps by the overwhelming size of the group. A highlight was the bursting of former Chicago Surface Lines car #1374, superbly restored by Frank Sirinek, out of a carhouse through a commemorative banner and into service on the streetcar loop. The final event was the visit to the Fox River Trolley Museum at South Elgin, where a parade of entirely different vehicles, including the 1890s Chicago trolley post office car, provided a fitting finale to the weekend.

People came to the CERA celebration from far and wide; one couple was there from Australia, others from Canada and England. Most noteworthy was the group of twenty-three members of COFEC, a Parisian counterpart of CERA, who planned an American visit around the Chicago event. It was a great pleasure to have them join us.

To develop and manage the Golden Anniversary activities, CERA directors (listed on page 5) formed a committee, including, from their ranks, Walt Keevil, Norm Carlson, Fred Lonnes and Stan Nettis. In view of the overwhelming task ahead, they also enlisted the aid of MCERAs Roy Benedict, John Darling, Ray DeGroote, Dick Hofer, Don Idarius, George Krambles and Art Peterson. Each accepted responsibility for one or more detail phase of arrangements.

CERA and the committee thank all who kindly wrote to comment on what a great time they had. It was especially enjoyable to meet with others from across the continent and beyond our shores to share interest in electric railways. We missed those who could not attend and hope they will be with us at future anniversaries.

Restored to its original paint job, Chicago Rapid Transit 5001 makes a trip during the CERA visit to the Fox Valley Trolley Museum.

Lineup of three generations of Chicago streetcars at Illinois Railway Museum.
—*Norm Carlson photo*